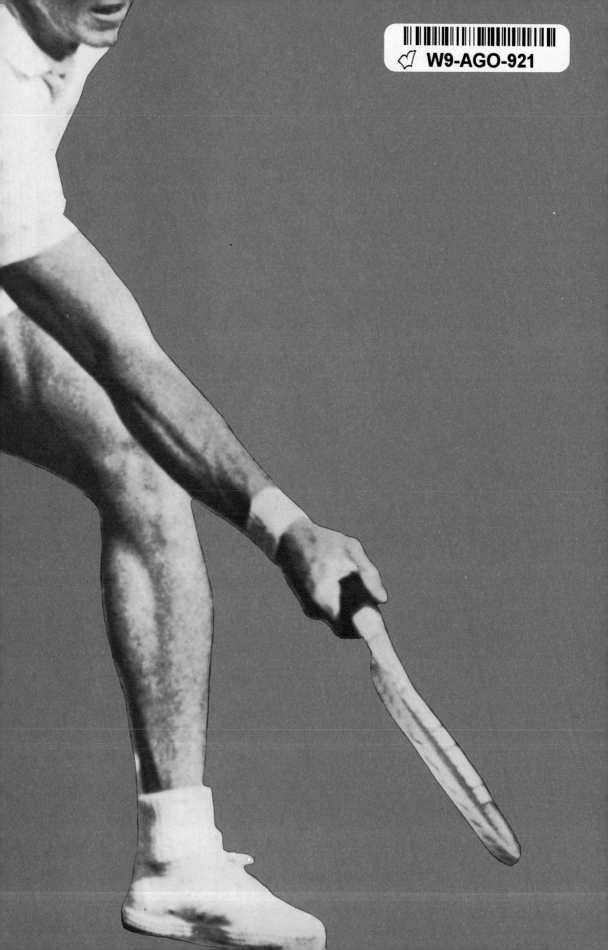
W9-AGO-921

Kramer
Rosewall
Gimeno
Gonzales
Hoad
Laver
Segura
Trabert
Sedgman
Budge

how to play TENNIS the professional way

EDITED BY ALAN TRENGOVE

Simon and Schuster, New York, 1964

First Printing

All rights reserved
including the right of reproduction
in whole or in part in any form
Copyright © 1964 by Alan Trengove
Published by Simon and Schuster, Inc.
Rockefeller Center, 630 Fifth Avenue
New York 20, N. Y.
Library of Congress Catalog Card Number: 64-12480
Manufactured in the United States of America
Printed by Reehl Litho, New York, N. Y.
Bound by Economy Bookbinding, Kearny, N. J.
Designed by Betty Crumley

ABOUT THE PHOTOGRAPHS

All the sequence photographs and some of the individual ones were furnished by Le-Roye Productions Ltd. and were taken specifically for this book.

World Tennis Magazine has been very helpful in making its photographic files available so that a few other photographs could be found to round out the illustrations. *World Tennis* supplied the photographs on pages 7 and 127.

Other photograph credits follow :

Page 113 (TOP)—P. W. Trostorff

Page 113 (BOTTOM) and Page 132—G. L. Kermadec

Page 117—Acme Photo

Page 135—Associated Press Wide World Photo

Page 144 (TOP)—A.A.F. Technical Training Command

Page 144 (BOTTOM) and Page 159—E. Peter Schroeder

CONTENTS

Jack Kramer
Foreword

Ten years ago professional lawn tennis as we know it now was in its infancy. It was always a very healthy baby, fortunate to be blessed with such fine progenitors as Bill Tilden, Bobby Riggs, Don Budge, Frank Parker, Dinny Pails, Pancho Segura and Carl Earn.

In December, 1952, the child had a transfusion that insured its growth into vigorous, competitive manhood. The Australians Frank Sedgman and Ken McGregor, who had captured the imagination of their own people and many others, turned professional after successfully defending the Davis Cup against the United States' challenge. Their signing was my first big venture as a professional promoter—I had changed status myself in 1947—and it was clear to me at the end of 1953, after a lucrative tour featuring Sedgman, McGregor, Segura and myself, that professional tennis was here to stay. The financial returns from that tour have never been exceeded, but each tour since has developed the professional game in some way, as well as insuring security for life for the players.

Now in 1964, with sixteen or so active great players on the lists, professional tennis can truly be said to have reached maturity. Some of these great players have written, in collaboration with Alan Trengove, a book that may well be described as a definitive work on lawn tennis technique. They are all here, all the champions of a decade and more, from Richard Gonzales to Rodney Laver. I am sure that a player of any standard will benefit in some aspect of the game from what these men have to say, for they have dominated the game for many years.

Each of them improved in skill after he turned professional. There are a number of reasons for this. First, as amateurs they were all imbued with tremendous will to win. They were proud champions when they moved into the more down-to-earth atmosphere of professional tennis, and the challenge they met there stimulated them. Second, they learned to think more deeply about what they were doing.

It is generally admitted that Jack Kramer's toss of the ball for the serve is probably the best in the game. Practicing the toss is one of the dullest of chores, but no one ever learns to serve like Kramer without doing so.

They might have won handily as the top guys in the amateurs, but when they joined me they had to analyze the game in general and each opponent's game in particular. They had to tighten up their approach, always seize openings, never play a bad game. They couldn't coast as they could in the early rounds of an amateur tournament, because every opponent was either as good as they or better. They learned the hard way that a professional is a player who makes almost all the easy ones and steals some of the tough ones.

It sometimes fell upon me to ease, as much as I could, the transitory stage from amateur to professional. Despite my doubts about his troublesome back, I had to prepare Lew Hoad, one of the greatest natural players of all time, for the war of attrition he would face against Gonzales. I took him on a six months' tour of Europe and the Far East, showing him that he couldn't expect to hit winners all the time against Gonzales, that he had to aim for consistency and eliminate errors.

A few years later another talented young man came to us, Andres Gimeno from Spain. Andres didn't win any of the world's big amateur titles, but as a professional he worked on his second service, and made his backhand and volley more aggressive. There is no doubt now that if he played as an amateur he could win any title he chose.

Not the least interesting facet is the way each player's personality has developed since he turned professional. No longer has he had someone telling him what time to go to bed, or what to eat and drink. He has had to make his own decisions, meet various newspapermen, appear on television and adjust his game to all sorts of conditions. Out of the additional responsibility has grown self-confidence. And yet, as his confidence has grown, he has had to contend on the court with the new champion from the amateur ranks, a champion normally unwilling to bow to anyone. It has made for intriguing situations.

The surprising thing is, I guess, that there are not more explosions among such deadly competitors. The rivalry between them is intense at all times, but rarely is there outright animosity. It existed to some extent between Gonzales and Tony Trabert in their 101-match tour, because they were somewhat incompatible. Mostly, however, the players have a deep respect for each other and get along fine.

Over the years they have played in all kinds of conditions—in suffocating indoor courts, in poor lighting, against white backgrounds and on unpredictable surfaces. If you have never played on a canvas court stretched over a rodeo ring, or on a court where the back wall is so close to the baseline that you can't make a backswing, you don't know just how difficult the game can be.

Such difficulties, plus the strain of incessant travel—the boys each travel up to 100,000 miles a year—demonstrate how thoroughly they earn their money. Remember, they are nearly all perfectionists, otherwise they wouldn't have got where they are. For a perfectionist, the circumstances in which these players sometimes find themselves can be very frustrating.

To some people it is puzzling how these fellows retain their zest for lawn tennis. After all, they are reasonably well off, maybe even wealthy, with wide business interests. But, remember, they love the game. They are born competitors. They are learning all the time. And the huge chunks of dough riding on the matches are a constant incentive.

In the pioneering days of professional tennis it was customary for me to sign on the top amateur and pit him against the top professional, either Gonzales or myself, in an extended series of matches. Only on one occasion since World War II, however, has the top amateur done better than the top professional, and that was when I managed to get ahead of Riggs. A situation could have arisen year after year, therefore, of the leading amateur turning professional, enjoying one profitable head-to-head tour, but then being killed off and lost to the game.

My plan soon became to enlist whole groups of players so that we could have various side tours and, most important of all, tournaments. As well as seeking the current Wimbledon champion, I brought into the professional game such fine players as Rex Hartwig, Mervyn Rose, Robert Haillet, Luis Ayala, Kurt Nielsen, Earl Buchholz and Barry MacKay.

There are now close to thirty members of the International Professional Tennis Players Association, including sixteen or so who are in tip-top condition and ready to play at any time in their best form. To keep them active, tournaments are organized around the world with commercial sponsorship. No one makes such a big killing as was possible from the head-to-head tours in the fifties any more, but on the other hand, every player is able to make a good living. Players who didn't win the Wimbledon title and who perhaps got beaten on their initial tour can, like Ken Rosewall, still make more money than others by dominating the main tournaments. This, then, is how the professional game has developed.

For many years I could see the day coming when, with such development, the players would have to control their own affairs, as the professional golfers do, and so in November, 1962, I retired as a promoter.

There was one other factor influencing my decision to pull out at that particular time. Some of the amateur administrators were claiming that I had a vested interest in the introduction of Open tennis, and that my aim was to run all tennis, amateur and professional. Although such accusations were ludicrous, I could see that possibly in the circumstances existing in 1962 I might be blocking Open tennis.

The International Professional Tennis Players Association thereupon took over complete control of the professional game. Through its capable Board of Directors, it deals with other organizations on an association basis. It is this association (and not any individual) that decides whether to guarantee a certain signing-on fee to the Wimbledon champion, and, consequently, every member has a stake in seeing that the game runs efficiently and smoothly.

I have no financial interest in the Players program, apart from a television series in which they play. But, of course, I'm always on hand to give the boys any help I can; you don't organize professional tennis for ten years without picking up a lot of experience.

One day I hope to see many of these fine players playing in Open tournaments. The present stalemate surely cannot continue, for the amateur and the professional games have much to offer each other.

Meanwhile, in this book, many of the greatest champions the game has known write about those special features of lawn tennis on which they are considered particular authorities. They have labored long and hard for the rewards that have come to them, and the enthusiasts who read and learn from this book will also reap rewards. It is a unique work.

Ken Rosewall

The Backhand

People watching a fast-flowing tennis match between leading players sometimes come to the conclusion that any similarity in the strokes unwound before them and their own strokes is purely coincidental. They see brilliant, unhurried strokes executed under pressure, and they despair of their own game. Why can't they improvise like that? Why can't they hit winners off the wrong foot?

Well, let's get one thing straight. Although the pace of top-class tennis prevents us from playing our strokes in the copybook manner all the time, we all appreciate that, given time to produce them, those are the best strokes to play.

I am a great believer in orthodoxy. It has done me good service, and as I was never endowed with outstanding physical attributes, I guess that I owe most of my success to my orthodox stroke equipment.

Orthodoxy doesn't preclude individuality. Some of the great champions of the past, such as Don Budge, Jack Crawford and Fred Perry, played immaculate strokes that would have satisfied the most demanding of purists, yet they remained individualists. In Australia over recent years youngsters have been coached en masse without being regimented, because the coaches recognize that natural flair can be crushed by rigid insistence on stereotyped preparation. But individualism isn't going to take a player very far if his preparation has obvious flaws.

Being pretty cautious—the other professionals didn't make me treasurer of our association for nothing—it's always been my contention that painstaking preparation plays a major part in making a champion. Naturally, agility and speed of foot are important qualities, too. Without them it's well nigh impossible to get very far. But preparation and the readiness to work hard in eradicating weaknesses separate the champions from those who never quite make that grade.

I may tell you that I've been playing tennis since I was knee-high to a grasshopper, and I'm still trying to do something about my weaknesses. It has occurred to me, for instance, that the reason my backhand feels more comfortable for me than my forehand is that unconsciously I prepare myself for the shot much earlier than I do for the forehand. It seems obvious that anyone who takes the trouble to drill himself in orthodox backhand preparation to the point where it becomes instinctive is going to achieve better results.

"Instinctive" is the key word. Once a match has started, it is virtually impossible to think systematically. Even the quickest thinkers can't hope to plot out their actions in the heat of battle. The match will be over while their minds are still ticking along. They can only practice along the right lines so that their responses carry them through in a match.

The majority of mediocre players feel that the backhand is an infinitely more difficult stroke than the forehand. They are able to dominate a rally only on their forehand and are ever ready to run around a slow shot to their backhand and take it on their forehand. As long as they adopt such an attitude they will always be mediocre.

Players who aspire to break into a better class of tennis must realize that they can't do it without a fairly efficient backhand, for once a weakness is detected on this swing it will be ruthlessly pommeled. Most of today's serve-volley exponents mold their whole game around an attack to the backhand, and, unless you can command some respect with your returns, you are going to be easy meat. The aim must be to build up strokes that win points as well as save them.

If it's any sort of encouragement to the battlers who are not too happy with their backhands, they should bear in mind that those who do play the best class of tennis and who, therefore, prepare their strokes properly, generally find the backhand a more natural stroke than the forehand. It is largely for that reason that this book opens with a discussion of the backhand, rather than the forehand.

The very fact that a good backhand can't be produced without a well-defined preparation means that fewer things can go wrong with it once that preparation is mastered. So if your backhand is shaky and you're not content to remain a no-hoper with it, make sure you are taking the right steps to improvement.

The first essential, as it is in any stroke, is a proper grip of the racket. Most of the best players, amateurs and professionals, use pretty much the same backhand grip, the Eastern backhand grip. Tony Trabert is one of the exceptions. He places his thumb along the back of the handle in the belief that this gives him more support. Trabert certainly has a fine backhand, but in my opinion it has its limitations in that sometimes he can be caught unprepared. Of course, if your wrist isn't very strong, you may find Trabert's device a great help.

My preference is for wrapping the fingers and thumb evenly around the handle and playing with a very firm wrist. Assuming you employ the Eastern, or "shake-hands," grip for the forehand, as most leading players do, give the racket about a quarter turn to the right. In a match, if time permits, the turning from forehand to backhand grips is done by the free hand on the throat of the racket. With this backhand grip, which is equivalent to the Continental forehand grip, you should be able to play any type of shot. It has always felt comfortable to me and I am confident in using it on any surface.

As professionals, we must adapt ourselves in switching from

board courts, on which the ball may skid through low, to clay courts, on which the bounce is high. My backhand grip enables me to be flexible in coping with any contingency. Playing on indoor courts I find that my preparation has to be completed more quickly than on the slower clay courts of Europe. Since the bounce on these clay courts is inconsistent, however, the preparation for the stroke is even more important than on other surfaces. As soon as a player knows the ball is coming to his backhand side he must try to adopt the correct stance, which is sideways to the net. The racket must be brought back smoothly and swung through to sweep the ball back over the net in a rhythmical, one-piece action.

Footwork is the secret of success in most sports. Don Bradman couldn't have hooked a cricket ball to the boundary without using his feet and Babe Ruth certainly wasn't flat-footed when he smacked a home run. For Bradman and Ruth immaculate footwork led to sweet timing. Had they not moved their feet into position they would have been unable to swing their bodies into their shots. And tennis players, like cricketers, baseballers and, of course, golfers, must have everything moving into the ball.

The size of a man isn't very significant if he lacks timing. On the other hand, the little fellows, like Neil Harvey and Gary Player, who time a cricket or golf shot exquisitely, can hold their own in any company. I reckon that at one hundred and forty-two pounds I must be one of the lightest men in world tennis, yet my timing of the ball has often enabled me to outpace men considerably heavier.

Now, when you see the ball is coming to your backhand you must shuffle your feet around so that they're pointing to the sideline. That's the first step toward good timing. The next is moving the right leg forward. Thus, in swinging at the ball you will not be cramped by your right shoulder and arm.

You must give yourself space in which to hit the ball with the arm extended, so if you have to run, try to judge your approach accordingly. Knowing at what distance from the ball to pull up and make the shot comes with experience, or, if you have extraordinary ball sense, instinctively. The top players take short, nippy steps and always have balance and control over their body speed. Watch how big fellows like Trabert and Gonzales move quickly and gracefully to the ball. Not for them the big, loping stride.

Practice moving swiftly about on the balls of your feet, ready to dash in any direction. And know how to withdraw the foot closest to the ball if you find yourself too close. The arm must swing uncramped from the shoulder, which is impossible if you are on top of the ball.

Remember that after you've wound back the racket fairly close to the body and the swing has commenced, the elbow must move out and straighten, unlike the action in the forehand.

As near to impact as possible, the weight is transferred from the left to the right foot. The right knee ought to be a little bent and relaxed, permitting the weight to flow into the shot. On the follow-through you keep balance by turning to face the net once again. Never lean back on the shot or you may loft the ball out of court. And never drag at the ball by having the hand in front of the racket; the ball is likely to curve viciously out of control.

At least 75 per cent of services are directed at the backhand, and when you have players like Gonzales pounding down the ball at one hundred and twelve miles per hour the stroke has to be pretty sound not to disintegrate. Where you stand in receiving service depends on the keenness of your reflexes and the power of the service. I usually stand no farther back than the baseline, lightly poised on the balls of my feet, leaning slightly forward and ready to move to left or right. On the second service I move two or three feet in.

I believe in keeping the backswing and swing-through as level as possible. This means that in returning service, especially a spinning second service in which the ball bounces higher, the racket head must be held fairly high on the backswing. It's useless taking the racket head back low when the ball obviously is going to bounce high, because at the last split second you'll have to make a hurried push upward in order to make contact.

The high backhand shot is, of course, one of the hardest to execute. Most players lack the strength on a high backhand that they possess on a high forehand, when the ball can be smashed away almost with a service action.

The same principle of bringing the racket back so that it doesn't have to "chase" the ball applies to the low and hip-high backhand shots. For the low shots you must bend the knees, bringing the back down low but straight. Above all, the racket head must be kept above the wrist when it is practicable or control will be lost.

The position of the ball in relation to the body is governed by the direction desired. If the aim is to drive the ball down the line it must be taken later; across court, a little earlier. Mostly it should be about level with your right shoulder.

A variety of backhands, some more effective than others, can be found among the top players. Lew Hoad and Ashley Cooper have powerful backhands, though I'd hesitate to advise anyone to imitate them. Due to the strength in his wrist and forearm, Hoad can hit a backhand with a high, top-spinning action, and when it comes off it's a very difficult shot to handle, the ball dipping through at high speed. At other times, say, when he's rallying from the back of the court, Hoad relies more on an orthodox backhand, slicing the ball for steadiness.

Since he turned professional, Cooper's backhand has developed along the same lines as Hoad's, except that his top-spin doesn't spring from any movement in the wrist.

My backhand is completely different from theirs, in that most times I slice the ball, striking it with the racket face tilted back. When I started playing tennis my backhand was flatter than it is now and I feel I can still hit a flat backhand if I want to, and sometimes, indeed, I do. My game is built around placement, consistency on shots and trying to outmaneuver my opponent. Lacking the power of other players, I have become dedicated to percentage tennis, because if I can keep the other fellow under pressure, making him feel he must constantly bring out great shots or have me dwelling on him, I'm going to win more matches than I lose. Hence my choice of a backhand hit with a slice action.

It is not, I must emphasize, a cut or a chop. They are bad strokes and I have nothing to do with them. I am still stroking the ball when I make contact with it. The reason that so much pace is imparted, even though the ball is sliced, is that my wrist is firm and I hit through the ball.

Quite a few players have contented themselves with chopped or chipped backhands in the last few years. Three who come to mind are Vic Seixas, Mervyn Rose and Neale Fraser. They've contrived to chip back a service to their backhand with a restricted backswing and follow-through, and then they race to the net, relying on their speed and volleying to make amends for any lack of penetration in the shot. These are very dubious tactics, and, in my view, a sign of weakness.

Nor do I favor merely blocking the ball on the backhand as some players do repeatedly. If a service is so fierce that all a player has time to do is block the ball, then he may be justified— it's better than not hitting it at all!—but blocking tends to make one lazy and overlook footwork.

Whether one should adopt my type of sliced backhand depends largely on one's grip. Trabert and Cooper have grips in which the hand is more on top of the racket and it must be almost impossible for them to hit a sliced backhand. They take the ball early and hit through it, but a low, quick shot to their backhand embarrasses them because they can't drop their rackets down low enough to hook the ball back into play.

I admit I give away some speed by slicing the ball and that what has worked well for me isn't necessarily advisable for other players. My aim is to control the ball and be able to be defensive. Trabert, Cooper and Hoad, because of their grips, find it easier to be aggressive than defensive. But aggression isn't always the right policy.

A sliced backhand enables me to have a greater variety of shots at my command. One of them is the defensive, short-angled shot. On a fast surface it is not always safe to play a shot like this, though if you have some touch and are quick-thinking, it's often worth trying as a stratagem that may confuse your opponent. Badly executed, it will set up an easy volley and lose you the point. I play the short-angled shot when the ball stays low in the middle of the court or, at any rate, somewhere near the service line. From this position it's not possible to hit the ball as hard with the normal strokes as from the back of the court, and if the opponent has advanced to the net it's not easy to pass him. Hoad has no problem here because of his top-spin action; nine times out of ten he will try to whip the ball past his opponent by sheer speed. For the more orthodox player, to attempt to unleash such power from mid-court is foolhardy, but taking the ball early and pulling it across on a delicate angle may unbalance an opponent. One warning: he will anticipate it if it's tried too often, and its effect will be nullified.

Taking the ball early, as it's rising, is a big advantage. No mat-

Ken Rosewall plays a classical backhand drive. With perfect footwork, he gets to position in plenty of time, right foot forward and right shoulder pointing toward the net. The racket is held firmly with its face a bit open, to give a slight slice to the ball. Notice that Rosewall watches the ball right up to impact, which is made slightly in front of his body. At impact, his weight has flowed solidly onto the right foot, and then his racket follows through in a smooth, sweeping action.

ter what surface I'm on, I always move into the ball on the backhand very early. The intention is the same on the forehand, but the result is not always as satisfactory. Obviously the rising ball is traveling at greater speed than the ball that has leveled out or is waning. Struck cleanly, as it's rising, its pace will be increased, giving the opponent less time to prepare himself.

I know many club players find it difficult to hit a rising ball, often mistiming it completely. It's worth persevering, however, because the ability to hit the rising ball is one of the things that separates the good player from the ordinary.

Only on social occasions do I attempt to top-spin a backhand. And the number of times I play social tennis in a year can be counted on the fingers of one hand! The top-spun shot simply isn't the right shot for me. If I tried playing backhands as Hoad plays them I'd finish up with a bad arm. His are practically table tennis shots, more suitable to his physique than mine.

Because the racket feels like a natural extension of my arm on my backhand side I can apply side-spin or under-spin and hit the ball flat on any angle or down the line without having to think of the technicalities involved.

Significantly, I feel that I watch the ball more closely than on my forehand. Watching the ball seems such a fundamental prerequisite of tennis that I hesitate to belabor it. But in most cases when I've seen a club match and been asked for an observation, I've had to point out that the players weren't watching the ball closely enough. The ball must be watched right onto the racket, and the temptation to lift the head precipitately to discover the result of the stroke must be resisted. Otherwise, all sorts of morale-destroying errors will occur.

I have explained that my backhand is better founded than my forehand. I should add that apart from all the constructive steps that go into its production, I have always found it easier when my right arm follows through away from my body than when I bring it across my body. No doubt others may not have the same kind of feeling, though it's interesting to note that most people do things like serving cards, and playing table tennis and hoop-la backhanded.

As a boy I favored the left side. I still throw a ball with my left hand and it was touch-and-go whether I learned to play tennis and cricket as a left-hander. When I whacked a ball against a brick wall for hour after hour, building up the good, firm wrist that's one of my chief assets, it was with my backhand.

Today, if the stroke is better than other players', it's largely because I can vary it so much. As an amateur it was even more outstanding in comparison with my other strokes, for in those days I didn't produce my forehand properly; neither did I exploit my speed in forcing the game from the net. The pundits placed me into the category of being a baseliner with rather a weak service.

It was expected, therefore, that I should play good-length drives until my opponent advanced. Then I should pass him. Unfortunately, like an actor who becomes typed, I myself became convinced that this was my natural role and did nothing to develop the more rounded game that I possess now.

As a professional, I attack at every opportunity. Most players prefer to attack off their favorite shot, and in my case I like to lean into my backhand early and follow it into the net. Sliced on grass, the ball keeps low. The shot may be across court, where the ball has more room over the lowest part of the net, or down the line. The shot down the line demands greater accuracy; if it's merely pooped high the opponent will move in and slam it away.

Sometimes it's possible to make an attacking stroke when in retreat. The most vivid memory that I have of any single stroke is one from my first Wimbledon tournament when Hoad and I were playing Gardnar Mulloy and Dick Savitt in the doubles. Hoad was serving and we had both camped ourselves at the net when we were lobbed. I chased the ball about fifteen feet behind the baseline, swiveled and slashed a backhand drive clean through Mulloy and Savitt, who were flabbergasted. The gallery nearly raised the roof off the stands.

This kind of shot has to be struck absolutely perfectly and some players—Segura, for example—simply lack the ability to whip it around. In the professional game we would be more apt to lob from such a desperate position, but a player confident of his backhand may go for such a winner. When he can pull it off ten times out of ten he has the kind of backhand that I would like to own.

Andres Gimeno
The Forehand

I remember the hot, dusty days when my father acted the part of one of those tennis machines that propels balls. He stood there, on the other side of the net at the Real, Barcelona, Lawn Tennis Club, where he is the professional, and knocked fifty or so balls at me, one after the other, for what seemed hours. I hit forehand after forehand after forehand. I sliced one, hit flat, put on top-spin. I played down the line, across court, lobbed. . . . Every forehand shot that had ever been thought of, and some that hadn't, were played on that court.

On school days my lunch hours were spent at the club slamming a ball against a wall hundreds, thousands of times, always with the forehand. My drive on that side came to be as instinctive as shoveling paella into my mouth, and this was as well, because it was to become my meal ticket.

Pancho Segura's two-handed fore-hand—often thought to be the finest single shot ever developed by any-one in tennis. Even at this stage, no opponent can be sure where Pancho intends to hit the ball.

Why didn't I work on my backhand to the same extent? That is difficult to say. For me, the forehand was tennis.

There's a saying that without a backhand a person will find tennis a hard game to play, but that without a forehand it is impossible. As a young amateur, my aim was to hit my forehand with all my might and go into the net, hoping my backhand would take care of itself.

Not until I turned professional did I feel any need to improve my backhand. For then, you see, the other competitors didn't give me much chance to show all the fine things I could do with my forehand, and I couldn't hurt them with my backhand. It wasn't that my backhand was such a bad shot, but being un-aggressive it didn't win many points. I had to do, shall we say, some homework on it. Now it is strong, though naturally not as strong as my forehand, and if I'm among the leading four pro-fessionals it's because my big forehand gets big results and my backhand is no longer defensive.

A visit to any tournament is enough to make one appreciate that good forehand strokes can vary enormously. Imagine the forehands of Pancho Segura, Lew Hoad, Malcolm Anderson and Pancho Gonzales, and you realize at once the possible range.

Segura's two-handed forehand is considered by most of us the finest single shot ever developed in the game, superior even to the backhands of Don Budge and Ken Rosewall, or to Gonzales' service. It may look unorthodox, but it is infallible. Segura cannot be put on the defensive if anyone plays into his forehand, because he can hit the ball hard or soft, play a drop shot or lob, and change the direction at the last moment, hardly ever making a mistake.

Hoad's forehand is also punishing. Serve wide to his forehand and he can flay the ball hard down the line or across court. A great many players, because they use a certain type of grip, can do one of these shots well but not the other.

Among the amateurs forehands differ even more. Although he was at his prime a little before my time, Gardnar Mulloy still basically has one of the best forehands, a fine, fluent and flexible stroke. His grip is something that I would describe as between East and West, enabling him to impart tremendous top-spin when he desires. He can also hit the ball very hard with great accuracy.

Some people think that, what with my open stance and my flourishing follow-through, my forehand is a little unusual, but I hope to show you that it is not only safe and sound; it is an attacking shot around which I have my built my whole game.

Let me first put forward simply the most important principles which the majority of textbooks fog by devious scientific instruction. To have a strong, forceful forehand you must take the ball sideways, almost as far from the body as you can reach, and you must take it as early as possible. In other words, don't let the ball come at or close to your body, and don't let it descend. Stroke it at the highest point to which it bounces, or better still, as it's rising. There are other intermediate forehand lessons to be learned, but if you keep these two principles in the back of your mind in shaping your general attitude, much of the rest will come easier.

One of the factors in producing a good forehand drive is the grip. Like the majority of leading players, I use the Eastern "shake-hands" grip for the forehand and can recommend it as the most suitable for applying controlled pace in all conditions.

Of course, there are different concepts of how a racket should be held, and I am the last person to insist that a young player should change an unusual grip if he finds it comfortable and reasonably effective. My own quirk is that I retain my forehand grip for my backhand, instead of turning the racket one-eighth to one-quarter in a clockwise direction as a lot of theorists say I should do.

When I was thirteen a Spanish coach said it was impossible to hit a firm, consistent backhand with a forehand grip, and he urged me to turn the racket, placing my thumb along the back of the handle. I said, "Look, you change my backhand grip and I quit the game." That was the end of such talk until Jack Kramer also tried to persuade me to make a grip change in my first year as a professional. Jack pointed out that Bill Tilden didn't become the greatest player of his time until he changed his backhand grip. But I resisted Jack, too, and improved my backhand in my own way.

Therefore, I will only generalize and say that the Eastern grip has been proved the best grip for most players on the forehand and that it is felt to be better when the fingers are stretched to cover as much of the grip as possible without discomfort. Pancho Gonzales and Earl Buchholz hold their rackets like hammers, however, and they've proved pretty fair tradesmen!

When you are waiting in the ready position you must have your racket pointing in the general direction of the net and not across to the backhand side, otherwise the distance you have to take the racket back is too far. Cradle the throat of the racket in your free hand, just lightly with the fingers, so that you are balanced and won't get a tired arm in a long match.

The sequence pictures of my forehand illustrate my full swing and the lusty follow-through that finishes, usually over my left shoulder. This action has been developed because of my wish to hit the ball with pace and top-spin. Being a tall, slim man, lacking the bull-like strength of a Hoad, I must throw all my body into the stroke to generate power. Hoad has a big wrist, but my wrist is normal and I must depend more on my shoulder.

Falling into a groove with a full backswing and follow-through is a good way of avoiding the jerkiness that wrecks many forehands. One warning, however: it is difficult to make a telling

The powerful top-spin forehand drive of Andres Gimeno starts with his early preparation for the stroke. While still on the run across court to the ball, he has drawn his racket well back. The racket head starts fairly low and comes through up onto the ball through impact. Gimeno's follow-through finishes high over his left shoulder. It is such a powerful, uncompromising shot that, as in this particular sequence, both feet are sometimes momentarily off the ground after impact.

shot with a full swing after the ball has leveled out and is dropping.

As the ball leaves your opponent's racket, make your move. Turning sideways to the net, start your swing with the racket parallel to the ground, pivot on your back foot (the right foot if you're a right-hander) and come through the ball transferring the weight onto the left foot.

Many players make the mistake of stepping across instead of toward the net with their front foot. As they make the stroke their bodies are twisted, they are fighting themselves, and they find it hard to pivot.

You will notice that I use a slightly open stance. I am half facing the net. Far from indicating a lack of body movement in the stroke, this stance helps me to pivot from the shoulders and hips more easily.

Being supple and loose-limbed is helpful, but if you feel you are not pivoting as well as you should, stand in front of a mirror and practice rotating the hips and shoulders to the right and back again. In my country the matadors do such exercises, knowing that their lives depend on their suppleness. What you must try to perfect is smoothness and rhythm, out of which will come power. It is no coincidence that many champions are also fine dancers; nor that the longest throwers pivot the hips and shoulders, moving their weight forward.

A forehand should be hit with a very firm wrist, though occasionally you will see some of the top players using a great deal of wrist to impart spin or for the sake of deception. I favor top-spin for a number of reasons. As the ball spins forward in an upward trajectory over the net there is a greater margin against error, and when it dips into the other side of the court it is not easy to volley or half-volley.

If you hold the racket firmly, start a smooth swing parallel to the ground and follow-through high, you will develop a fine top-spin shot. Naturally, you must bend at the knees and waist for the low shots so that you won't be forced to drop the head of the racket too far.

Don't have your feet too close together, or you won't have a firm base; you will lose balance. On the other hand, if the feet are too far apart you will find it hard to recover and move off quickly for the next stroke. Footwork plays the major part in perfecting balance and timing, which in turn determines whether a player makes heavy shots. A small man timing the ball in the middle of the racket can hit far heavier shots than an uncoordinated giant.

Nowadays, whenever anybody serves to my forehand and I see the ball in time I hit it as hard as I can, hoping for a winner. My faith in the shot is complete. Nine times out of ten, if I go for a big hit on grass or cement, I win the point. It is very satisfactory having such a shot that opponents fear, for they cannot hide from it all the time.

Most players would, understandably, consider it rash to go for winners whenever the service is to their forehands. Their methods of dealing with the service must hinge very much on the court surface and the quality of the service.

There are three possibilities. First, the ball can be hit straight down the line, a stroke that is difficult to counter, but often for some players equally difficult to execute. Second, the ball can be top-spun at a fine angle across court, putting the incoming receiver under considerable pressure. Or third, the ball can be driven low directly at the opponent as he comes in.

The third possibility is not as weak as it may seem. If the first two possible returns are made a little inaccurately you can be in a lot of trouble. For instance, when the cross-court return is a bit high or not angled enough it opens up your own court. You must try to run and cover the court, but your opponent may either volley the ball into the open space before you get there, or volley it back from where you have run. Either way, you probably will have to make a hurried stroke—if you get to the ball at all. But by returning your forehand hard and low at your opponent you are cutting down his chance of angling his volley and you may be able to play a forehand winner on the next shot.

Never, if you can help it, merely block the ball on your forehand return of service. Although the ball may be traveling extremely fast, try to make a stroke at it, shortening your backswing if necessary. After all, if you are hitting winners off more than 50 per cent of the services you are not doing too badly, and blocking is not going to put any pressure at all on your opponent.

My favorite forehand is the ball hit across court with top-spin, which usually either beats a player or forces him into error. For most players the cross-court shot is easier to execute than the shot down the line, and one of the giveaway signs of a weak forehand is an inability to stroke the ball with any pace in that direction. Too often you see the ball steered with a chipped action.

With the shot across-court the ball is struck up to two feet in front of the body, whereas the shot parallel with the side line is made approximately one foot in front of the body. The secret of the side-line shot is to hit a fraction later. It is necessary to have a command of both cross-court and down-the-line shots, because, no matter how strong your favorite shot, you will not gain the maximum benefit if you rely too heavily upon it.

There was a classic demonstration of this lesson at Wimbledon in 1963 when my fellow countryman, Manuel Santana, the number two seed, was surprisingly defeated by Fred Stolle. Manuel was considered to have the finest forehand in amateur tennis, and this might have been so. But a big factor in Stolle's win, it seemed, was serving wide to Manuel's forehand because he discovered early that invariably the return was diagonal, and he was fairly certain from where he would have to volley the ball.

An effective cross-court shot against a net-rusher, of course, is the one dipping past his feet, forcing him to grope and volley or half-volley upward. I use it a lot on fast surfaces.

On slower hard courts, where there is more rallying from the base line, greater depth and placement is required. It is not so easy to go all-out for winners on hard courts, because the ball bounces higher and slower off the court and more maneuvering is required.

On grass and boards the ball comes through fast and low and you may have to take a shorter backswing; with a firm wrist you use the pace already on the ball. On cement the bounce is still fast, but you must be prepared to swing higher. However, the Eastern forehand grip, with the face of the racket slightly open coming into the ball, functions well on all surfaces.

Hard-court tennis, by which I mean tennis played on clay or en-tout-cas, is a different game from that played on other surfaces. It is well known—painfully well known—that hard-court players rarely do well at Wimbledon or in the later stages of the Davis Cup competition. The only hard-court country to win the

Davis Cup is France, whose players—Cochet, Lacoste, Borotra and Brugnon—were among the all-time-great champions a few decades ago, but, since the war only Petra and Drobny of those raised on hard courts have won the Wimbledon singles title.

Europeans say that grass is for cows. They are brought up to play slower, more guileful shots, to rally and move their opponents around, waiting patiently for an opening before going to the net. They do not place such importance on the service as grass-court players, who develop powerful services and follow each ball into the net.

For all their artistry, players such as Manuel Santana and Nicola Pietrangeli, who formed their strokes on clay, are handicapped in the big grass tournaments, for they don't instinctively serve and go to the net, even though they have adapted themselves to do this with experience.

Many Europeans slice the ball, a bad habit. Perhaps one of the reasons that I have done well on grass and boards is that never did I resort much to slice, except on my backhand. Never did I slide to the ball, as a lot of Europeans do, and merely push it back. I ran to it and hit it. When I started to play on grass, and then on indoor courts, I realized that if I sliced the ball the shot would be dead. So I kept on running and hitting. The slice, the chop, or whatever it may be called, is not basically a good shot, except maybe when the ball is short and fairly low. Then it can be taken early, sliced low and deep into the backhand corner, giving you time to reach a dominating position at the net. The shot may be safer than the hard-hit drive from mid-court unless you are very consistent. But if you play it badly and the ball falls short you are vulnerable.

It is worthwhile watching the champions to see when and how they play these strokes. In my own case, Jack Kramer, Pancho Segura and Dinny Pails visited Barcelona in 1949 when I was a lad and I'm sure by watching them I improved my game. For one thing, I could see the advantage of having top-spin for both defensive and aggressive purposes.

When you are trying to build up a particular stroke, go along to watch a champion, forget the spectacle of the match and concentrate on watching him solely for minutes on end. And don't be afraid to ask questions. Most of the leading players are happy to answer questions and give advice to any of the lads who show promise and enthusiasm.

One of the hallmarks of a strong forehand is the ability to change the direction of the stroke at the last fraction of a second. Nothing is more demoralizing than to be caught running the wrong way, and you will quickly break a player's confidence in attacking the net if you can fool him with your passing shots.

Disguising direction comes with experience and I don't think anyone should attempt it until he is playing a high standard game. One way of disguising your shots is by a little flick of the wrist just before impact after you have noticed, from the corner of your eye, that your opponent is trying to anticipate. But using the wrist in strokes entails a risk.

Another means of deception is altering the relationship of your body to the net and the opponent. In other words, you step across a little further to indicate that you are about to play the ball down the line, but you turn on it early and hit it across court. The trouble is that by changing your mind like this you may be too clever for yourself and make errors. On the whole, it's safer to decide quickly where you want to hit the ball, to prepare your shot properly and to make it as good as you can.

Disregarding the disguising of your shots, what are the ways you can eliminate any weaknesses your forehand may have and build on its strengths? Almost all good forehands are top-spun and I suggest you work to develop top-spin without using your wrist. Try to develop a stroke in which the racket head comes up from below the level of the ball and, after contact, finishes above it. Lew Hoad and Rod Laver have been successful with wrist action, but both are exceptional athletes of great ability. The average person will get into difficulty and become jerky in his action if he tries to use the same amount of wrist as this pair.

Work for depth, consistency and accuracy. Check your stance and the way you step into the ball, making sure that at contact your weight is coming through the shot.

Good forehands sometimes collapse overnight, one reason being late preparation for the stroke. Players run to the ball on their forehand side keeping the racket out in front, instead of moving it back as they run. Consequently, when they arrive at the ball, instead of the racket being in a hitting position, it still has to be brought back for a hurried swing. The stroke is bound to be inaccurate and possibly extremely wild.

All good players, even if they don't have to run, prepare early, getting the racket back with their weight on the back foot and stepping into the ball, with knees a little bent and wrist firm.

Some of the best players—Tony Trabert, for instance—find it more difficult keeping their eye on the ball right up to impact on the forehand side than on the backhand. And it's generally agreed among the professionals that, because the body tends to play a restricting role, a forehand can disintegrate more easily than a backhand. After taking the racket back, there is nothing to guide the arm and the racket, and any of many things can cause a breakdown. It is a good idea, therefore, to have a mental checklist like that of an airplane pilot, so that if the stroke does break down you can run through the list looking for the trouble —taking your eye off the ball, late preparation, too much wrist, or whatever it may be.

Confidence means so much to all of us, and even an experienced tournament player can have such a bad run of losses that he loses confidence in his forehand. Maybe he is seeing the ball later, he's anxious to avoid risks and tries to play safely. Under pressure, he attempts to steer the ball. But he has the "wobbles" and loses control. If he is trying desperately hard to win matches, he will worry. The forehand will go from bad to worse until finally he is in a bad state.

My advice to such an unhappy player is to go out and hit the forehand freely in a match as though it were only practice. While he is fretting, he will be unable to concentrate and play positively. So hit out. Remember, it's impossible to win all matches. Anyone with ability and keenness will win his share of matches if he keeps stroking freely and confidently. If I played one hundred matches a year I'd be happy to win eighty.

Mixing of pace is something to aim for at all times. It is important to have accuracy with shots of all pace. You may be involved in a rally with a solid driver who is thriving on pace. You are not worrying him at all. A slower ball, perhaps a half lob, may break up his consistency. He will have to think a little, change his stroke, make his own pace. It may be difficult for him.

Accuracy and subtle changes of pace, added to my regular

hard forehand drive, helped me to achieve one of the best per-
formances of my amateur career when in 1958 I was making a
private tour of Australia. I played Barry MacKay in the Victorian
championships at Kooyong at a time when Barry was keyed up
in an effort to play himself into the United States Davis Cup team
for the Challenge Round. Rain interrupted the match and it was
spread over two days, but we both concentrated well and turned
in an exciting game. My forehand was in such good order that I
won in five sets, a victory that aroused the interest of Jack
Kramer, who was in the stands. My forehand also got me big
results at Queens Club in 1960, as my wins over Raman Krish-
nan, Rod Laver and Roy Emerson convinced Kramer that I was
professional material.

A few critics considered that I left the amateur game too soon,
but I felt, and I think rightly, that there was more chance of improving as a professional. As it turned out, I learned more in a
few weeks while getting beaten twenty-one matches to seven by
Pancho Gonzales than I did in years as an amateur. But I was
gratified to realize that even the great Pancho respected my
forehand.

Richard Gonzales

The Serve
and How to Vary It

Picture in your mind a chain reaction in which the body moves into the ball, the shoulder moves into the ball, the elbow extends and the wrist snaps through the ball. There, simplified, you have the service action. The power comes from the coordinated speed of the action.

In modern lawn tennis the emphasis has shifted increasingly on to big serving, and it is not easy to recall a champion in recent years who got by without a powerful service weapon. The advantage of having a big service is in the pressure it puts on one's opponent. As the match progresses he begins to fear that if he loses his own service it will cost him the set. The strong server may also be able to conserve more energy than his opponent by winning his service games more easily. He should be more confident of his condition lasting in a long set or a long match.

I concede that the possession of a big service alone isn't enough to become a champion. A player needs other strokes as well. But a player with an outstanding service and fair ground strokes has the foundation for a successful career.

Early in my own career I relied a lot on my service, my ground strokes being only moderate. In the final of the United States singles championship at Forest Hills in 1949 it was my service that saved me and enabled me to beat Ted Schroeder. Not for another two or three years, until I played many matches on clay courts, did the rest of my game improve. To survive on clay courts you just have to have sound ground strokes.

In my time I have played against many players with great services. Probably the greatest was Jack Kramer, who hit the ball very hard (his service was timed at 110 m.p.h.) and was extremely accurate and deceptive. Frank Sedgman is another good server, with a consistently hard first service which he follows with tremendous speed into the net to volley away winners. Lew Hoad has a hard and deceptive service that has always presented me with difficulty. Barry MacKay, because of his height, can send down balls at terrific angles and has great power. However, he usually directs his service to the backhand, and though it travels at high speed, it is not as difficult to handle as the more deceptive services of Kramer and Hoad. Bobby Riggs was a small player, but he accurately served to the corners, pulling his man out of court. Another hard and baffling server was the Czechoslovakian-born left-hander, Jaroslav Drobny, now a naturalized Briton.

In the average match, 50 per cent of points are won by serves, the rest by volleys and ground strokes. There admittedly are traps in making such generalizations. A person like Kenneth Rosewall might win only one point a game on his serve, and the rest by volleys and ground strokes. On the other hand, I might win three points a game with my serve and only one with volley and ground strokes. It all depends on the strength of the player's service. But obviously if it's possible to win 50 per cent of points by service the stroke deserves at least 50 per cent of your effort to perfect it.

My serve was natural from the very beginning. I had one coach, a high school coach by the name of Spears, who told me that if I threw the ball up a little higher and a little farther behind my head I would get more spin on the ball. Following his advice, my serving improved almost overnight.

At home there is a guy named Charles Pate, three years older than me, who has done more to remind me of my faults than any other player I have ever known. If I am serving badly he invariably can put his finger on the fault. He will come over and tell me what I am doing wrong; usually I'm not throwing the ball high enough and not reaching for it.

In all these years of lawn tennis, years in which I have managed to beat off many players' challenges, I have never become overconfident with my service. I have practiced my serve just as much as, if not more than, any of my other strokes. Sure, you have to practice on your weaknesses. But you mustn't overlook practicing your strength. Your game will always be built around your strength.

Let me tell you how I serve. My grip, which is orthodox, is very important. It's almost the backhand grip, but perhaps not quite all the way.

In singles I stand about six inches from the center line when serving into the deuce court, and about two feet away from the center line when serving into the advantage court.

The stance for each service is exactly the same, thus increasing the deception. One of the big secrets in serving is in disguising the delivery in order to keep the opponent off balance.

The flat serve is hit by snapping the wrist and opening the face of the racket just as the ball is hit. I aim the flat serve primarily to the backhand corner, and, being right-handed, I follow through on my left side.

For the slice serve I swing the racket away from my body, hitting around the ball and again following through on my left side. The ball is thrown up about nine inches in front of my forehead (though higher, of course) and into the court, so that I have room to hit around it. The slice is used for drawing the opponent out of court, especially if he has a weak forehand, and it is effective on grass on which the ball stays rather low. It is an offensive shot, used in the top company almost as much as the flat serve.

The twist serve is hit by dropping the head of the racket behind the back, then swinging up and over the ball. For this serve the

Richard Gonzales' flat serve cannonballs at you at 112 miles per hour. A smooth, coordinated action sees the body coil and the toss made. Notice, in frame 5, the extent to which Gonzales' body comes into the shot. His weight is almost totally on the left foot, his eyes on the ball throughout, and his follow-through comes swinging down to its finish on the left side of the body.

ball must be thrown behind the head, and the follow-through of the racket is high and to the right of the player's body. The twist, or American twist, as it is often called, is mostly a consistent serve used as a second serve, because it clears the net comfortably and cuts back into the court with a greater margin of safety.

Incorrect tossing up of the ball in serving causes as many errors as any other one factor. You must practice and practice and then practice still more to synchronize the toss of the ball and the swing of the racket.

The position of the ball in the air varies by two, three or maybe four inches between the first serve and the second serve. You throw it to a height about an inch or two beyond the point you can reach with your racket. At the ball's zenith you go up on the toes of your left foot, stretching as far as you can in striking it.

On the first serve you should hit the ball just at the moment it starts to fall. On the second serve the ball can be allowed to drop two or three inches before you go up to meet it. From this position you will be able to impart the spin which will bring the ball into the court. Because the back has to be arched in order to get spin on the ball, the twist serve is the most tiring of all. Otherwise, I have found that big serving doesn't necessarily use up undue energy.

Whether a player should go flat out for a cannonball on his first serve depends largely on the quality of his opponent. A flat serve bothers some players more than the spin serve. You must react very much like a baseball pitcher, varying your serves to keep the other guy off guard and off balance, but serving mostly to his weakness, whether it be the forehand or the backhand. Sometimes the court surfaces are inferior and it may pay, therefore, to make sure your first ball goes into play by sending over your second spin serve first. Then you can hurry in and command the net position.

While the second serve cannot be quite as severe a weapon as the first serve, it can be more aggressive than most players make it. Practice the second serve by hitting it deep and to the corners. That will give you confidence. Your first serve will be as good as your second serve allows it to be. If you are sure that you can hit a second serve without double-faulting, you will get more of your first serves into play. But the knowledge that your second serve is poor will make you miss more first serves through fear of double-faulting. You have to work on that second serve to make it as consistent as it possibly can be.

Before serving you should stand relaxed behind the base line, bouncing the ball once prior to beginning your windup. The left foot ought to be planted firmly by the base line, two to three inches behind it, with the left shoulder pointing toward the net.

Your body must move freely as you transfer the weight from the ball of your left foot onto all of the toes, which bear most of the strain as you reach up for the ball.

Do not hesitate on your forward motion. The tendency to fall into the court is perfectly natural and is part of a good service. As you fall forward you regain balance and are ready to move off in any direction for the return. Normally, in regaining balance you take one step into the court, occasionally two, and these steps ought to be made quickly to prevent being caught in the middle of the court on a deep shot.

Rhythm comes with practice. The service is a continuous motion from start to finish, and if you relax and swing freely you ultimately will fall into a rhythm.

I like to see players taking their time with their service, analyzing their action and trying to do something extra with the ball. Outwardly, they should go through some ritual of approaching the base line and bouncing the ball in the same way each time. That will help them to get into a groove.

But while they go through this drill they must be thinking. They must put thought into their second serve, using their first serve as a guide. If the first ball was too long, the racket must be brought into the ball sooner to pull the second serve down. And if the first serve finished in the net, the racket has to be swung farther out to carry the second ball deeper.

Most of the time when I'm serving I try to penetrate my opponent's weakness. Normally, the more his weakness is attacked the more errors he will make. Once in a while, however, I will serve to his strength in an attempt to stop him from getting set for one particular shot. I do this especially on my second serve.

People can remember that over the years Pancho Segura was devastating with his forehand, and yet, throughout my career, I felt I won many points serving to his forehand, simply because he crowded his backhand, opening up the whole of his forehand court. It was a calculated risk which a lot of players wouldn't have taken. It is very dangerous playing into as great a shot as Segura's forehand.

Too many players follow their serves into the net irrespective of some factors that should discourage them. You must assess your serve and your opponent's ground strokes before gambling everything on a rush to the net. If your serves are falling short it is suicidal to follow them in. You must wait for the ball on which you can be more offensive.

The other guy's return of service may be extremely accurate. In that case you'll have to wait longer and try to maneuver yourself into a more aggressive position. Of course, you may have no ground strokes at all. Then you haven't much choice: you are safest at the net.

Wind and sun can pose problems for players of all standards. I wish I knew the answers. The only attitude to take on a windy day is to concentrate harder and make allowance for the strength of the wind. In serving into the wind, naturally you have to hit harder to get the ball deeper. Hitting with the wind, you ease up on your shot, allowing the wind to carry the ball to a good

depth. It's not a bad idea to shorten the service action. There will be less risk then of mistiming.

As for finding yourself looking directly into the sun when serving, all I can suggest is that you adjust your stance to the right or the left. The fact is that the wind and the sun, and all other weather conditions, affect both players. Accept this from the start. Try to use the conditions to the best of your ability, and don't allow them to upset you. What it really comes down to is strength of character.

Some players feel that confidence in the whole of their game hinges mainly on their serving. I don't know why this should necessarily be so, unless all they have is a big service. Confidence, to my mind, comes from hitting the ball in the middle of the racket and executing winning shots.

But I agree that a bad spell of serving in the middle of a match can break a player's morale. If he can't get his first serve into play he becomes that much more apprehensive. What ought he to do?

Well, he must concentrate more and look more intensely at the ball. Sometimes a player will take his eyes off the ball before it is struck; this is the cause of numerous faults. He must stretch

Gonzales throws the ball a little to the right and in front of his forehead in order to execute the slice service. Notice, too, the position of the racket face at impact—this imparts the slice. Gonzales is serving into the first court and hitting around the ball to force his opponent out of court on the forehand side.

up for the ball at its highest point as he swings. And, if necessary, he must ease up on the power. It sounds obvious, but many players don't seem to realize that you must get the serve in to have a chance. A slower serve is better than a cannonball that never goes in.

Be careful of foot faults, which occur more frequently in club tennis than is generally realized. The most common foot faults are usually caused by lack of concentration—perhaps by a player unthinkingly walking up and stepping on the line as he serves. If you form a habit of deliberately placing your left foot two or three inches behind the base line you will avoid this.

Other foot faults are caused by the left big toe, as it bears the weight, turning onto the line; by the left foot creeping onto the line; and by taking a small, steadying step onto the line. These faults can be eliminated if you step back as much as four to six inches behind the base line before serving.

I doubt whether I have been foot-faulted more than a dozen times during my career. My left foot is very firm. I know that I can place it within half an inch of the line without risking a foot fault.

When I started playing the game the rules forbade the back foot from crossing the line before impact, and I must have been foot-faulted about a half dozen times on this clause. I solved the problem by stepping back six inches. Now, of course, the rule doesn't operate.

Height is a great advantage in serving, for it allows a player to hit the ball with greater angle. A tall man has this extra angle and he can hit the ball harder with a greater margin of safety.

The smaller man has to put spin on the ball to get it to hook into the court. He thereby loses power. Two small men who've developed great serves are Rod Laver and a player of the past, Bobby Riggs. Jaroslav Drobny, whom I've already mentioned, wasn't too tall, either. Lew Hoad, who has a fine serve, is five feet, eleven inches, but most of the best servers are at least six feet. I stand a little over six feet, three inches and Barry MacKay is about six feet, four inches.

Change of pace in serving is often worth a few points. The receiver may be standing a foot or two behind the base line waiting for the fast first serve. A slower, spinning ball may catch him by surprise and give you a little more time to close in on the net.

If, however, he has quick reflexes and a strong return of service you are taking a risk. He will be away ahead of the ball, unworried by the change of pace.

One of the curious aspects in many long sets between two good servers is that finally, when there's a break, the other player breaks back immediately. Although it causes excitement in the gallery, it shouldn't really happen. The player who has the set in his grip by breaking through first either relaxes from overconfidence or suffers a mild letdown. The pressure has built up while the games were going with service and when, after sustained effort, he takes his opponent's service, he has a nervous reaction, missing volleys that up till then he's been putting away. The answer is to concentrate harder, move in more quickly to a volley and watch the ball like a hawk.

When you get into this position of having victory within your grasp you must call on all your "killer" instinct and try to close out the match without the loss of a point. Don't relax on the first point when you are serving at 5-4, 9-8 or whatever the score is. Move in immediately and close out the set as quickly as you can. Then concentrate even harder in the second set, because overconfidence and lack of concentration will automatically become a hazard, causing you to drop service early in the set.

So often your strategy in serving must be governed by the state of the game and the ability of your opponent. At 5-4, for instance, you might feel that it's important to get to the net more quickly, so you serve a little more slowly, providing yourself with more time in which to go forward and make a sound volley.

It pays always to be offensive with the first service, because an attacking delivery gives you two chances of winning the point. But in a tough match, when I can see my opponent is tired, I may try to conserve my energy by discarding my cannonball and making sure my first serve goes in. The fact that he is weary means that my opponent will have just as much trouble returning a consistent first service—even though it lacks my full power.

A number of present-day players have developed the habit of holding only one ball when they serve. I cannot see any merit in it. Most players can hold two balls in one hand quite comfortably, and with practice, it becomes easy to retain one ball while throwing the other into the air.

Those who keep one ball in the pocket of their shorts may be

The twist serve imposes tremendous strain on the back and stomach muscles. Here, left-hander Rod Laver, who serves one of the most formidable "kickers" in the world, demonstrates the upward-and-outward action of the racket. He tosses the ball over and slightly back of his head, bends his knees, and arches his back to get down under the ball. As Laver whips his body into the service, his racket moves outward as it moves up and over the ball with wrist snap. The action carries Laver forward at impact, and a moment later he is poised and balanced, despite the contortions of the twist service, ready for his opponent's reply.

creating a pressure on a leg muscle, causing them to get cramp or tire that particular muscle much faster than muscles in other parts of the body.

As for throwing one ball aside when the first ball is good, I don't know that it is fair to the opponent. Some umpires rightly have ruled interference when this has been done.

New balls in a match, or balls that become wet and heavy, demand added concentration. It is an advantage to have new balls to serve, because they travel about one-tenth faster. A wet, heavier ball will drop as much as five or six feet shorter than a dry ball. One has to concentrate on hitting through it with the center of the racket in order to get it deeper.

It shouldn't be beyond anyone to develop a strong service as long as he sets out observing the right principles. Women have more difficulty because they are not as strong physically. A little girl is more content playing with dolls and dresses and helping round the house than in building up her muscles. Boys meanwhile play sports such as baseball, basketball and, in Britain, cricket, in which they use a motion that can be incorporated later into a tennis service. Consequently, when they start playing tennis, boys find it more natural to serve than girls. And, of course, they have stronger forearms anyway. Wrist action, as I have said, is important in generating service power.

All of us in trying to improve our service will occasionally serve double-faults. They needn't be discouraging. I have served many in my time, not because of a fault in my swing or any nervousness, but through aiming for the lines and the corners. I have great confidence in my service and I figure that going for the lines pays off. Don't, therefore, be distracted by double faults, if you are trying to play boldly.

Finally, never serve in a lazy manner when practicing. Serving hard over the years will develop those muscles that are used in serving. Practice as often as you can, hitting your serves to the corners and lines, and slicing the ball off short to the forehand. Have confidence in this and every other serve so that in a match you know exactly what you can do with each ball. Your game will grow accordingly.

Lew Hoad

The Volley

The volley is more often decisive than any other shot in tennis. Backed by a strong service and speed about the court, it can carry an amateur player into the final of any major championship.

Most clubs have members who are instinctively good volleyers, yet unimpressive from the back of the court. On a more exalted level players like Bob Falkenburg, Ken McGregor and Vic Seixas have carved a niche for themselves in Wimbledon and Davis Cup history by their prowess with service and volley, though their ground strokes were relatively poor.

I am not suggesting that players these days should develop the volley at the expense of their ground strokes. The greatest champions are those who can play all the strokes with equal certainty. But, whereas a moderate champion may be able to get by without outstanding ground strokes, he is lost without his volley.

In a tough, five-set match between a volleyer and a player who operates mainly from the base line, the volleyer must have the edge. It is less exhausting rushing to the net than crossing from side to side in a prolonged base-line rally. The baseliner may be in the ascendancy for a while, but if the volleyer can extend him to a fifth set the baseliner's game will suffer the most from weariness. He will find the gaps that the volleyer leaves at the net increasingly elusive as fatigue robs him of his accuracy.

Some players are so steady from the base line that only a relentless volleyer can crush them. Give them room to dictate rallies with their line-splitting ground strokes, and they take a grip on the match.

John Bromwich was such a player. His uncanny ball control mesmerized many an eager serve-volley exponent. I fell to him once in the New South Wales championships when he tied me in knots with his tantalizingly soft but tellingly placed ground strokes, and bundled me out in three sets.

Herb Flam, with his peculiarly effective strokes, was another tricky customer for the volleyer to beat. The net rusher must be right on top of his game to get the better of clever players like these. But beat them he can, provided his volleying is strong and he doesn't relax the pressure by going to the net behind weak services and poor-length ground strokes.

Volleying, like smashing, is frequently strenuous and spectacular. To be a brilliant volleyer, a player needs some flair. He must be well coordinated and flexible. And he must have a quick eye.

I was lucky enough as a boy to be able to volley well without giving any great thought to what I was doing. The ball came over the net and I laid into it with all my might. Maybe occasionally in those early days my lusty hitting went a little astray, but it was the only way I wanted to play.

It wasn't until I was well launched on my amateur career that I started to ponder over the mechanics of volleying, and in the last few years I've had to modify the technique that came naturally to me as a boy.

The greatest lesson that I've absorbed as a professional is the importance of reducing my backswing on the volley. A comparison between a group of amateurs and professionals will show that one of the chief differences in style is in the backswing.

The danger of having a long backswing is that it increases the margin for error. When the racket has to travel farther before making contact with the ball there's always a chance that the ball won't be struck in the middle, especially if the volley has to be hurried.

Even Rod Laver tends to take the racket back too far when the ball is just above the net, resulting in those wild shots which the critics describe as "inexplicable." Weighing only 150 pounds, the Queensland redhead no doubt believes that he needs a big swing on the volley to generate power. Less accomplished and heftier players than Laver can be seen winding up and following through so prodigiously that they're off-balance when their opponent returns the ball quickly.

I have found that the volley made from a short backswing is safe and still decisive from the greater control that I'm able to achieve. The pace of the shot is governed by the length of the follow-through; the direction, by a turn of the wrist at impact.

Another difference between the amateur and professional lies in what is attempted with volleying. As an amateur I used to volley hard into the corners or up the center of the court. Like other lads, I was taught the center theory—that if you volley up the center you restrict your opponent's angle for passing you.

This is sound reasoning up to a point, but for the first couple of years in professional tennis, in which many of the competitors were at least as good as I, I found a lot of my best volleys being fired back.

To hold my own, or even survive, I had to angle my volleys, not necessarily applying as much pace, but striving for finer subtlety. The volleyer who can stand in the middle of the court and angle his volleys confidently to within a few inches of the lines will generally have the better of the game.

This advice, of course, is for the advanced player, who is not concerned with the rudiments of volleying. And so for the less advanced, before I go any further, I will outline the rudiments.

At the outset, remember the ball must be watched closely and the body kept loose and relaxed with the knees bent. The racket

Keeping his eye closely on the approaching ball every second, Lew Hoad runs across court for a finishing forehand volley. His firm grip keeps the racket head poised and up. Using a minimum of backswing, he punches the ball, his weight flowing through to his front foot. Hoad has met the ball well in front of his body, which is almost at right angles to the net. The follow-through controls the pace of the shot—this one is clearly punched away for a winner.

should be level with the flight of the ball and, if possible, the handle parallel to the ground.

On low volleys particularly the body must go down in a crouch so that the head of the racket isn't dropped. Control is maintained by a firm wrist.

The volley on both sides ought to be hit in front of the body, in contrast to the forehand drive, which is hit in line with the body or at most barely in front of it.

Don't wait for the ball. Be aggressive, go forward and punch it with a locked wrist. You have gone to the net with the object of winning the point quickly, so don't concede any of your advantage by a lack of boldness. You ought to be moving forward as you volley, not standing still, and certainly not retreating. The more you are moving forward the better your chance of connecting when the ball is higher and hitting it down.

Footwork is almost as important for the volley as for ground strokes. Being closer to the net, there is less time to move into position, but ideally the body should be at right angles to the line of flight of the ball. For maximum power, the left foot comes forward for the forehand volley; the right foot forward for the backhand.

The footwork is most essential on the backhand, for without the right shoulder pointing to the net the volley will lack pace and accuracy. When there's insufficient time to move the feet, at least try to swing the trunk around from the knees and hips. As is the case for ground strokes, you must step back with the foot nearest the ball when your body is in the way.

In championship tennis, especially doubles, the ball travels to and fro so quickly that the orthodox stance can't always be adopted. We often have to volley off the wrong foot when we are stretched out wide. This is difficult enough when it is unavoidable to deter us from making a practice of it on all volleys. Balance helps us to negotiate these awkward shots, and if you study good volleyers you'll see that they use their free arm to achieve balance. They also make for the middle of the court after each volley and here again the free arm can help in changing direction.

The angle at which the face of the racket is held on a volley depends on whether the ball is taken high, low or at medium height. For a low volley naturally the racket face must be slightly open to loft the ball over the net. The open face gives the ball some under-spin, aiding control, which is of more value than power.

But if the ball is above the net the racket face may be closed. The racket is held above the wrist in order that the ball can be struck down, either with a slice, a clipped flat hit or a drive-volley.

The drive-volley is brought into play when the ball is traveling rather slowly on a high trajectory and the opponent is clearly on the defensive. The shot requires a long backswing, which is warranted in these circumstances only.

Neale Fraser's forehand drive-volley is one of the most devastating in world tennis, though in his early days it used to be erratic. One of the temptations in trying to slam the cover off a ball which is invitingly high, and coming slowly, is to take your eye off it. Then the ball may be crashed over the base line or even the back fence. Neale used to do this quite a lot, but now he is not so overanxious and his drive-volley is deadly.

Speed and the stamina to maintain speed for a whole match are useful assets for the serve-volley game. A player should be on his way into the net as he completes his service. If it's his first service he should be able, by running flat-out with short steps, to reach the service line as the other bloke is about to return the ball. At the service line he must be able to pull up and maintain balance until he picks the direction of the shot he has to deal with. The quicker he anticipates the better, for then he can dart off to left or right as need be. When he makes the volley he should be six or seven feet inside the service line. Hence the need for speed and flexibility.

It must be stressed, however, that speed is of no advantage unless it's controlled. A footballer sprinting down a field has less chance of side-stepping a tackler than a man who is running three-quarter pace.

Similarly, the server who hurls himself at the net without check finds it difficult to change direction when the ball is returned down a sideline or sharply across court. But provided he makes the service line comfortably, he's in a handy position to pick off the return.

If it's a slow ball hit short across court he can either dash

Lew Hoad moves in and crouches low for a backhand volley. His knees are bent, his right shoulder points toward the net, and he is beautifully balanced. Notice, in frame 4, Hoad's firm grip, holding the racket head up solidly just before impact. He is very close to the net, so he has to open up the face in order to loft the ball over it, but this has been a controlled shot all the way.

in and volley it or take one step backward and make a ground stroke. Players like Rosewall, Segura and myself also resort a great deal to the half volley, which the average player ought to shun, but which is invaluable to us in high-pressure tennis because it reduces the amount of court we have to cover.

One of the objectives of the volleyer is to make the other man half-volley as often as he can, as it is almost impossible to make a winner out of a half volley. If you can keep your opponent trying to dig the ball up you are doing a good job. The low volley, say ten to twelve feet behind the net, is one of the most exacting shots, and there aren't too many players who can play it and consistently win the point.

Coming to play the low volley, you must drop down to a crouch by bending the knees. Unless you do, you won't get a good look at the ball. It may finish anywhere.

Small men, I suppose, have an advantage here, because it is less of an effort for them to get down. The Italian, Orlando Sirola, measuring six feet, seven inches, provides a classic example of how not to play the low volley. He ambles to the net in a leisurely gait and pokes his racket down without any "give" in the knees. For such a big man he has superb touch and so he usually escapes not too badly scathed. But his haphazard low volleying is a real weakness and limits him.

I have not mentioned the grip until now because it is not something on which I am well qualified to give advice. Had I learned the game properly I would have an orthodox grip. The professionals have subjected most aspects of the game to analysis and we've discovered, among other things, that usually the players with good, orthodox forehand grips produce the best forehands, and those with good backhand grips produce the best backhands.

I'm accustomed to telling young fellows not to take any notice of me but to go to an accredited coach and learn the right grips from the start. That's what I would do if I were learning the game all over again. I'm a freak because I use the same grip for everything—ground strokes, volleys, service and smash. The lot. My grip is something between the Eastern forehand and backhand grips. It's only because I have an exceptionally strong arm and wrist that I get away with it.

Most of the top players volley with the Continental grip in which the "V" formed by the thumb and forefinger lies astride the inner edge of the handle. This grip enables them to make all types of volleys without shuffling the racket about.

The strength in my arm and wrist was developed by gymnasium work when I was a junior. Without it, I could never whip my top-spin shots so severely or thump my high backhand volley. Most players can't do much with a high backhand. It's a bit of a strain swinging the racket high up on that side, especially if you're a foot or eighteen inches off the ground. Brawn comes in handy.

Anybody who wants to build up that brawn and be capable of playing "wristy" shots like mine—and I'm not sure that they should—must be prepared to do a lot of hard work in the gym. Even if they don't play shots like mine, a strong wrist is a big asset in tennis anyway. If you have the patience and will power, I recommend regular sessions of manipulating a weight. Sit down and rest the forearm along the knee so that the wrist hanging over the knee joint bears all the strain. Move the weight up and down and from side to side. You will soon notice your wrist strengthening.

I have to admit that Rosewall hits his backhand volley as well as anybody and that in his case the pace comes from perfect timing. He keeps the head of the racket high and his wrist firm. With a short, controlled backswing, he judges the ball nicely, relying on a little under-spin for accuracy.

Some players look as though they're never too sure what they should attempt to do with their volleys. I have said that I have had to resort to more angle, but often, of course, it's not practicable to go for a winner. It may be all I can do to volley deep. No longer do I try to pulverize the ball, though I certainly volley hard, because soft volleys lead to trouble. Generally, a firmly hit good-length volley is sufficient to put pressure on an opponent. He still has to pass me to win the point, and maybe, as he endeavors to do so, I'll go for the angle.

Jack Kramer perfected these tactics. If he volleyed deep into the backhand corner and had his opponent on the run he knew that the most likely return was up the line. Kramer was ready for it and knocked it off for a winner. He could afford to guard less against the angled return when his man was stretching for the ball because most times it wouldn't come off.

When I was still a junior, Frank Sedgman was the Davis Cup hero of the day, and though when he turned professional he was outgeneraled by Kramer's percentage tennis, he is one of the greatest volleyers I've seen. Sedgman uses the wrong grip for the forehand, but he's so quick about the court and so assured on his forehand side that he leaves an opening of two or three yards to tempt his opponent to hit down there. Then he swoops on the ball and, so help me, whether it's six inches or six feet above the ground he invariably pulls off a mighty shot.

Gonzales is another wonderful volleyer. He never misses. Like Kramer, he punches the ball back deep, knowing that it requires a really good shot to deprive him of the point. The big fellow never really pounds his volleys. He hits the ball way out in front of his body with heartbreaking accuracy. In his prime there was no way he could lose the point when he wanted it badly. He would make sure his first service was right, then hit a safe volley and cover the obvious reply.

Left-handers often look spectaular, but in my experience they're not as sound volleyers as right-handers. Jaroslav Drobny, for example, had a basic weakness on his forehand volley. He found it natural to drive the volley like his forehand ground stroke. To do this he got over the ball. Most players would find this kind of shot difficult to control, but Drobny's quick eye and hard hitting enabled him to get by. Had he played regularly against the top professionals, however, the shot would have broken down.

Fraser has a fine, vigorous forehand volley that seldom fails. On his backhand he can't punch his volley away, and he relies more on slice and deception. On the other hand, Art Larsen possessed as perfect a volley from both sides as anyone could hope to see. Undoubtedly unconventional in many ways, "Tappy" was absolutely correct in grip and footwork.

Among women players there have been and are few good volleyers, in spite of the fact that it's been demonstrated by girls like Althea Gibson, Karen Hantze Susman and Margaret Smith that aggressive net play pays high dividends. Although women can't move as fast as men, there's no reason why they should be so timid and tentative when they venture to the net.

How can anyone improve his volleying? The best way of strengthening any stroke is by going out and playing fellows who are better. Unless it's a tournament, don't try to hide weaknesses; expose them, work on them. Be prepared to spend a couple of hours practicing one stroke if necessary.

In Australia, Davis Cup teams have become accustomed to pep up their volleying by intensive sessions at the net. Three players go out onto the court with two or three dozen balls, two players taking volleying positions on one side of the net, with the third on the other side. Then they volley away, trying frantically to keep the ball in play. Half an hour of quick-fire volleying like this, with the players alternating positions, helps to make volleying instinctive, no matter which foot you're on. You'll also find you can scarcely hold the racket up afterwards! The Australians in the professional troupe still practice volleying in this manner.

Ever since I can remember, Australia has had good volleyers, the reason being perhaps that two of the men with the greatest influence on the game there, Harry Hopman and Adrian Quist, were outstanding volleyers themselves. I can't think of one player selected for our Davis Cup teams for the last ten years or so who wasn't a fine volleyer, though there have been several with suspect ground strokes.

There are various refinements to the volley, which the ambitious must try to add to their armory. A few players who find that they can execute these refinements rather well tend to overdo them to the detriment of their over-all game.

The drop volley comes into this category. This is a touch shot that ought to be attempted only when the opponent is at the back or wide of the court and has little chance of reaching the ball. It can be particularly effective on wet grass courts on which the ball dies, or against opponents whose physical condition isn't one of their strengths. Played too often against anyone fleet of foot, it can be disastrous.

The drop volley shouldn't be played off the hardest drives, unless the ball looks as big as a pumpkin, because the timing needed to take all speed off the ball has to be just right. It's no good telegraphing your intention, so the motion of the racket ought to be virtually the same as for the normal volley, except that at the last fraction of a second the wrist is turned. The racket face slides under the ball, which drops lifelessly, we hope, over the net. If it bounces with back-spin toward the net, so much the better.

Gonzales is a master of the drop volley. Not only does he open the face of the racket, but at contact he brings back the racket with the artistry of a sleight-of-hand expert. Even if you can play the drop volley as superbly as Gonzales, however, play it sparingly.

The lob volley is another shot for the touch specialist. The odds against its succeeding are so great that we professionals only try to bring it off in doubles when, perhaps, we are having the worst of a rally and we are caught with a low ball while our opponents are in a threatening position eight or nine feet from the net. Again the racket face is opened. The ball is hit into the air as deeply as possible in order to give the volley lobbers time to recover. If the opposition has any class at all the chance of lofting the ball over them and confining it in court from a volley is pretty remote.

My advice is to content yourself with developing a dependable volley without frills and giving it a lot of work to do. Spectators lament the advent of the modern serve-volley game because they think it's spoiled the rally, but unless the rules are changed or the pressure of the tennis ball reduced the volley will remain the "killer" shot of tennis. The same spectators would protest just as loudly if this weren't so.

Rod Laver
Advantage Left-Hander

Left-handed tennis players, like curvaceous sweater girls, have a built-in advantage. If they have more-than-average talent they can achieve spectacular triumphs, simply by being left-handers. But they also have built-in disadvantages, which, if not overcome, can keep them struggling ineffectually in the bottom ranks. I should say that the advantage of being a left-hander outweighs the disadvantage, although, as I am the only left-handed player currently appearing in the professional tournament game, I may be biased.

Many left-handers seem to carry within them the seeds of their own destruction, and I must count myself fortunate that this has not been my fate, too. On the other hand, it might have been that I was in better hands than most at the start of my career.

My biggest slice of luck was that nobody ever tried to persuade me to play tennis right-handed. Up to the time I went to school in Queensland the majority of Australian education authorities compelled lads who were naturally left-handers to switch hands, despite the fact that they lacked coordination with their right hands. This policy applied not only to ball games, but to writing, and every other sphere of school life. From what I can gather, the frustrated boys lost confidence. Inability to play ball games with any degree of success was the least disastrous result of the insensitive bullying they were subjected to. In some it brought on a stammer. Others developed all sorts of inferiority complexes. It could well be that if I had been born a few years earlier I might have been told to persevere with a racket in my right hand and never have got anywhere.

Everyone—my family, my school and my coach—encouraged me to play lawn tennis as I wanted to, as a southpaw. These days I can't believe that any boy is forced to use either hand against his will, because in all sports left-handers possessing natural ball-control and rhythm have proved that the highest rewards can be theirs.

Why anyone should find it easier to use his left hand is beyond me. No other member of my family is left-handed (my sister used to be left-handed, but without anyone pressuring her, she switched to the right), and in double-handed sports, such as cricket, baseball and golf, I take a right-handed stance. I can receive tournament checks with either hand!

The consensus of opinion among knowledgeable lawn tennis supporters is that while left-handers are often brilliant, they lack much of the solidity of the champion right-handed players. Left-handed wizards, such as Norman Brookes and Art Larsen, so the feeling goes, are the exceptions to the rule. Most left-handers break down under pressure, especially on their backhands. I must admit that there is some basis for this contention, but I also maintain that proper coaching can insure that a left-hander's ground strokes are rocklike in reliability.

His big, inherent weakness (the seed of destruction within him) is his tendency to slice his backhand. I guess I could have finished up with a sliced backhand like anyone else when, as a youngster, I started playing with my parents and brothers on our outback farm. But my family took me to an excellent coach in Charlie

Hollis, who taught me to perfect a flat backhand. I made a low backswing, met the ball with a flat racket face and followed through high. Such was the humble beginning of the distinct top-spin action I have developed since.

In those days it was not a swift top-spin action, but it was enough to help me gain control. I got to the stage where off the backhand I could hit a flat stroke, a flat-slice or top-spin, and gradually I became increasingly more attracted to top-spin. I watched the other players, Lew Hoad particularly, and noticed what spin did to the ball, how it made it behave when the ball bit into the court.

Some players—Don Budge and Ken Rosewall for instance— have great accuracy with their backhands. I haven't—at any rate not the kind of accuracy that would enable me to hit a post with a drive nine times out of ten as a few of them can. But the top-spin takes care of much of the accuracy for me. I can forget about distance. I can hit the ball with top-spin three, four or five feet above the net and know that if it's straight the ball will fall into court.

Other left-handers, instead of stroking the ball with a flat action or hitting up and over it as I do, jab at it. They don't get their shoulders around at the ball. They don't take a full swing or have any rhythm. And their footwork is awful.

I have seen many left-handers poking at the ball with bent elbows in a halfhearted way that can only bring about their downfall. Against moderate opposition they may survive, but against players with penetrating services, ground strokes and volleys, there is little hope for them.

Neale Fraser was one who, for much of his career, didn't get his left shoulder down to the ball as he should have. Most of us on the tournament circuit try to help each other, and so once I pointed out Neale's backhand fault to him. Immediately he started to hit his backhand much better. He remembered to place his feet in the correct position so that his back was almost facing the net, and he made a full swing, pivoting from the hips.

If every left-hander in the doldrums, with sliced backhands curling out of court, endeavors to move his shoulder round and down to the ball he will make considerable improvement. Mervyn Rose had the typical left-hander's cramped backhand. Every top-

Unlike many fine players, particularly left-handers, who slice their back-hand drives, Rod Laver belts it with top-spin. The result is one of the most devastating strokes in big-time tennis. Notice that on the approach, Laver swings his left shoulder around until his shoulder blades are not too far from being parallel to the net. He takes a firm, pronounced step forward with his left foot, giving himself plenty of freedom to make his swing. There is no cramped look about the Laver backhand. The upward flow of the racket and the long follow-through impart top-spin. (All directions would be reversed, of course, for a right-hander.)

class player he met made it a target, and Mervyn never really worked on a remedy. Neale did—and all the game's highest honors were his.

Because of my top-spin, my ground strokes are far from classical. This doesn't cause me to lose any sleep. By top-spinning the ball for so long I have built up a strong wrist, which, along with the left-hander's normal ability to apply more spin, has helped me enormously.

Top-spinning the ball, I find that when I'm in trouble I can slam the ball a little harder. In a tight match this has a relaxing effect. The more I hit out the more I loosen up, and the other fellow probably finds it disconcerting.

But I'm not against cool, classical ground strokes if that is a player's game. It all depends on one's coach. Charlie Hollis was a terrific coach for me. He took me over when I was eight or nine and taught me the fundamentals. A lot of coaches cannot go beyond the fundamentals, but Charlie knows all there is to know about lawn tennis, and when I was twelve or thirteen he rounded me off, allowing me at the same time to incorporate my own idiosyncrasies in my game. I recall his basic teaching: a low backswing, hitting through the ball, developing a groove with good, strong strokes; sticking to the right footwork, front foot moving out to the ball; bending the knees as far as possible, taking the backswing back quickly; moving the racket straight back behind the ball; keeping the backswing flat and following through; a high backswing for a high ball, a low backswing for a low ball. That's how Charlie taught me, and how, I'm convinced, the game should be taught.

My first games were on an ant-bed court on our Queensland farm. As a hard court, it was not very immaculate, but all the family enjoyed their games on it and it was certainly helpful in my development, as I feel that hard courts produce the more skillful players.

My best wins have been on grass, but hard courts demand a greater variety of strokes and are my favorite surface. On grass an inferior stroke player can keep an opponent at bay by means of a big service which can't be returned as it zips off the court. The other side of the picture is that so many of the clever European hard-court players lack the speed, strength and reflexes to cope with the best grass-court players. They can't be beaten at home; at Wimbledon they can't beat an egg.

Grip? Well, at thirteen I used the Eastern backhand grip, with my thumb along the back of the handle. A few years later I found this restricting, and I modified my grip to bring my thumb around by the inside of the handle. My grip over the last few years has been the same for all strokes, a virtual Continental grip, a compromise between the most popularly accepted forehand and backhand grips. It has evolved naturally, and hard-and-fast rules on the kind of grips young players should adopt and keep in spite of discomfort would appear to be unwise. I guess the conventional grips, Eastern forehand and backhand, are the safest for lefthanders, bearing in mind the tendencies to slice. But once their strokes are formed they should not be afraid to adjust their grips to their growing repertoire of shots.

Some left-handers don't seem to appreciate the psychological advantage that they enjoy in playing the game "the wrong way round." The proportion of left-handers to right-handers must be very low, a fact that helps us significantly. In most clubs righthanders play most of the time among themselves. Their reflexes become attuned to the right-handed game. Then they're thrown on a few, infrequent occasions against left-handers. The ball comes from a different angle. It spins in an unexpected direction. Unless players have plenty of experience, it may take them a set or so to get used to this unusual behavior of the ball. They may never get used to it.

Right-handers are grooved to attack the backhand, but against left-handers they must direct their shots to what in an orthodox match would be the forehand. The top tournament players can swing their attack to either wing without embarrassment to their games. But lesser players can be excused if they're confused in the heat of battle and inadvertently attack the left-hander's strong forehand.

All these factors are in our favor, plus the fact that most of us are pretty lively players, happier at the net than on the base line. On our day, with our spinning services and unusual volleys coming off, we have a chance of flustering opponents.

Don't ask me why left-handers serve so well. I think all the left-handers whom I've known have had good services, even if they didn't reach top tournament standards. Just think of Jaroslav Drobny, Neale Fraser and Mervyn Rose. Their services formed a huge part of their games.

Left-handers obviously can slice and top-spin the ball viciously. A few right-handers, perhaps, can slice the ball as well, but they may not be able to top-spin their services at all. And not only do we southpaws have a flair for spinning our services, we invariably control our services better than any other strokes. The lesson is this: We have a natural advantage at the start of every service game—like a sprinter receiving a yard start—and so we should make the most of it and work on our services until we have the utmost confidence in them.

Nobody could do any better than study Fraser's serving action. Has there ever been a more formidable left-handed service in the game? Before, with experience, he improved his other strokes, it was often Fraser's big serving, allied with his lionhearted courage, that won him matches. He would be love-40 or 15-40 down in a crucial game and still pull the game out of the fire with a succession of unplayable services. For some reason or other, I don't mind playing left-handers or facing their services. Fraser's was the toughest I had to play as an amateur and it didn't really bother me. I admire his action, however. It is the only one I have ever tried to copy, in any phase. I tried to throw the ball up as Fraser does in order to disguise my services. He can throw the ball up in an identical way each time and hit a top-spin service, a kicker, a sliced service or a flat service. It is almost impossible to pick them until they're on the way, and much of his success is achieved by this element of surprise. I have worked on the problem for the last two or three years, but still I can't disguise my services to the same degree as Fraser.

The other important features in Fraser's serving are his stance and weight control. He is beautifully balanced to get all the power and devilry flowing through his action, and his weight control coming through to the ball cannot be improved upon. So if you take my tip you'll try to learn from the way Fraser serves. I did.

Fraser is, incidentally, the only left-hander who ever gave me much encouragement on my way to the top. He was the only one I looked up to. He was a few years older than me, he had greater experience, he was a tremendous fighter and if he had anything to say I listened, although, of course, most of our strokes were totally different.

Playing Fraser is a different experience from playing anyone else. He has a big, whipped forehand, a poky-type backhand, a big service and volleys that are more effective than they appear to be. He knows all there is to know about strategy, and with his irregular shots he is an extremely awkward opponent. For a long time I was faced with a psychological barrier when playing Fraser. It wasn't until the 1960 Australian championship final on a hot, steamy day in Brisbane that I defeated him for the first time. He led two sets to love and I scrambled out of the third set, 8-6. My physical condition gave me the edge in the final two sets, but it was touch-and-go until the last point. That victory removed the psychological barrier and in the next two years I won fairly well against him.

Of the main left-handers in my time I rank Fraser behind Drobny and ahead of Rose and Billy Knight. All four were masters of courtmanship, particularly Rose, who had more tricks than a cage full of monkeys. But none really enjoyed sustained pressure on his backhand.

Where I benefited on my way up is that I *relished* opponents playing to my backhand. While the others groaned at having their backhands played by a powerful hitter, I had the initial grounding in hitting my backhand flat or with top-spin. The more it was attacked, the stronger it became. In my last few years as an amateur I had controlled top-spin on my backhand, and an easy, natural forehand that, like most left-handers, I could disguise quite effortlessly. Opponents didn't know which side to attack and, if they chose the backhand, I had no doubt about its cracking. That, in a nutshell, was how I was good enough to achieve the Grand Slam.

One of our hazards is that we make more use of our wrists than orthodox players, which means we can be brilliant, flicking away devastating shots as though we were on a squash court, or we can be terrible and compared unfavorably with right-handers who keep their wrists rigid. I have enjoyed playing spectacular, wristy shots since I was a young boy. As I have pointed out, my wrist is strong now and I have control. And when playing somebody for the first time, it is he who is uncertain.

So long as you are basically sound, it is a matter of flair how you hit a tennis ball. To me, it would be extremely difficult to perfect a flat shot and hit it time after time with reasonable accuracy, although most coaches try to teach their pupils to do this. I would be lost without top-spin, which I first experimented with on my forehand as a schoolboy. Even in the professional ranks I have found the boys troubled by a lot of top-spin shots. The professionals are used to the conventional—such as Rosewall's flat forehand and flat-sliced backhand—balls that I, at any rate, find quite easy to volley. A player has to watch the dipping top-spin shot very closely, however, because even though he has it well covered he can make an error on the volley.

My game has been compared with Lew Hoad's. Hoad was my idol as a teenager, and I think I admire him now as much as I did then. But I certainly didn't try to imitate him. It doesn't pay to imitate anybody. You can learn from him without imitating. He has evolved his game, making use of his own particular flair. Unless you are identical twins, you are unlikely to share exactly the same flair.

Lew and I are similar mostly in our approach to the game. We are both products of the power era. We hit the ball powerfully, and the more power you pile on, the more care you must take in accuracy. Hence our top-spin. But Hoad isn't as wristy as I am. He doesn't hit the ball with a floppy wrist. He has a really tight wrist and comes up over the ball, while I, especially on my forehand, wrap my wrist around the ball a little more. Superficially, we resemble each other in our strokes—but mainly on the backhand. Our real similarity is in our free-hitting attitude to the game.

I have made the point that I don't think much of a sliced backhand, but, of course, I deliberately slice the ball sometimes when approaching the net. The object is to provide a fraction of a second longer in which to take up the net position and to keep the ball low when it lands.

As the ball spins backward it lingers in the air. There is an opportunity of getting set at the net instead of still being on the move when the ball is returned, whereas the top-spin ball travels faster, will "sit up" when it lands and may be hit with more angle. As a means of approaching the net, therefore, the sliced backhand can be recommended—but never at any other time.

The best and most satisfying way of improving all these strokes is in competition. Practice matches provide perfect opportunities to experiment with new shots while still maintaining the feel of competing against another player and pacing oneself. As for team practice, Harry Hopman used to have all his boys on court together. Two of us maybe would be at the net, one on the base line and two or three would be allotted the task of picking up the balls. The action was fast and furious, the fellow on the base line hitting any shot he wished—lob, passing shot, dink shot, anything. The two players at the net would try to volley to the lines, out of the baseliner's reach, so that he had to run to the ball and had a tough time keeping it in play. Such teamwork in practice develops keenness, team spirit and stamina.

Are left-handers outstanding volleyers? I don't think so. Volleying is an integral part of their games, yet forceful left-hand volleyers are few and far between. They have good touch, they generally anticipate well and they are deceptive. Their volleys lack the depth and power of the best right-handed players, however. Fraser was a deceptive volleyer, who often defeated fundamentally better volleyers at Wimbledon because he wrong-footed them.

It is because of their deceiving touch volleys—and their serving—that left-handers make such useful doubles players. The combination of a mercurial left-hander, such as Fraser or Rose, with solid right-handers of the caliber of Ashley Cooper and Rex Hartwig can be devastating. In the case of Rose and Hartwig, it was Hartwig who created opportunities for Rose to scintillate at the net or overhead. Mervyn's touch always made him a menace.

As a rule, a left-hander who pairs with a right-hander should play in the left-hand court. The pair will feel more comfortable lined up this way, and will be very strong on the outsides. They will be a little more vulnerable down the middle than the usual partnerships, but with experience they can make up for that.

A left-hander who plays in the left-hand court alongside a right-hander of the caliber of Ken Rosewall or Roy Emerson is very fortunate indeed. Rosewall and Emerson have strong backhands that can deal with anything down the middle. They can also return the ball exceptionally well off the forehand.

If the left-hander has a reasonable backhand, he should have every chance of breaking service. Off his backhand in the left-hand court, the left-hander should be able to dink the ball away from the net man, sometimes whip it across more aggressively and sometimes lob it.

It's not often that you see a left-hander playing in the right-hand court. This arrangement may confuse the opposition for a while, and it's strong down the middle, but it carries dangers that make it injudicious for club players. On grass, for instance, the ball travels so fast and low that a left-hander in the right-hand court has a terrible time trying to reach a service sliced to his backhand. If he does barely reach the ball he cannot get over it. It's all he can do to slice it back. Then a volley is fired back low again to his backhand. One way and another, he and his partner are likely to be in deep conflict.

There's another disadvantage. Most left-handers have longer backswings than right-handers. In the right-hand court, when they're moving in for a possible interception on the forehand, they're vulnerable to a ball going straight to the body. They are hard put to move their feet or the racket quickly enough to dig the ball out.

As an amateur I once played in the first court to allow my right-handed partner, Bob Mark, scope to exploit his fine, sweeping backhand return of service. We did moderately well, though the arrangement was never really satisfactory.

In 1962 I again played in the first court, this time partnering another left-hander, Jaroslav Drobny. We won the British hard-court title, as well as other titles in Sweden and Norway. One of the big factors in our success was that Drobny had wonderful control of his backhand while his forehand, of course, was extremely strong. And the sight of two left-handers volleying at the net seemed in itself to bewilder some of our opponents.

I make all my volleys with the one grip, my normal Continental grip, and on both sides I tend to hit a flat-slice shot. Rather than wait for the ball to meet the racket, I punch at it, keeping my wrist firm. A tight hold on the handle is essential, as is watching the ball closely to insure striking it with the middle of the racket. The head of the racket has to be held at an angle of anything up to forty-five degrees above the wrist. The other things to remember are moving quickly to the ball, bending the knees to get down to it, and behind it, and limiting the backswing. I am only now starting to reduce my backswing, which has caused me trouble against the hard, low drives of the professionals.

My game, in fact, has shown an encouraging all-around improvement since I turned professional after the 1962 Davis Cup Challenge Round. The improvement is due largely to playing such wonderful exponents of the game as Rosewall and Hoad. At first, I wasn't sure whether I had made a wise decision in turning professional, because in the early matches they were completely on top of me. I had never before met such unrelenting pressure. Had I not tightened up my strokes I would quickly have gone under. My first and second services weren't strong enough to make them extend themselves, and their returns of service made it hard for me to volley well. To survive, I had to serve better and jump into the net faster.

Now my ground strokes and volleys are sharper, and I have shortened my backswing in order to cope with the fast court surfaces.

There is still room for improvement, mostly at the net. In this company my volleys are not sufficiently penetrative. To be able to apply pressure on the top professionals a fellow must be able to volley the ball fast and deep into the corners. Then he may have a chance of volleying the returns for winners. After several months as a professional, my volleys are still a bit short.

Lack of concentration certainly doesn't worry me as it used to. A professional who doesn't concentrate 100 per cent of the time is inviting defeat. Early in the tour, when we were playing eight-game sets, I discovered that if I lost concentration for even a few seconds I would invariably lose the set. Maybe I would double-fault or hit a loose forehand volley or make a couple of bad returns. That would be all they needed to tie up the set.

In my younger days, playing somewhat aimlessly through one minor tournament after another, I occasionally lost concentration to such a degree that I had no idea of the score. What a contrast there is between my attitudes then and now! In professional tennis it is imperative to know the score all the time, because it determines your tactics. If you have got the break and you lead 30-love, you don't go for the big shot, hoping optimistically it will take you to 40-love. No, you play a good, sound shot in an effort to put pressure on your opponent. You let him make the errors. So, what with the tougher competition, the importance of being aware of the score, and the constant incentive of securing a nest egg for the days when I can't play tennis, I'm positive my concentration is better than ever before.

Not that it was too bad in my last year as an amateur. Then it was the ambition to achieve the Grand Slam of major tennis titles that made me concentrate. In the big events victory meant too much for me to allow my mind to wander.

An interesting thought is whether the speed of modern travel, which enables the world's leading players to cram in so many more tournaments than in the old days, helped me or hindered me. When Don Budge won the big four titles—the Australian, French, Wimbledon and American—he traveled the world at a much more leisurely pace. Probably, he didn't play in half the events that I did in 1962. I have come to the conclusion that it was an advantage for me to have played tennis almost incessantly throughout the year, although admittedly in some ways I was "over-tennised." The fact is that it would have been more difficult having a letdown for a week or so and then having to build up again for each big title. I was able to keep my confidence up by winning the smaller tournaments while playing at about three-quarter pace. Then when the big ones came along I knew I had the form. Since my first tour overseas the excitement of competing in the big tournaments has always given my game a sharper edge, and so it was in 1962. As for Budge, he must have been such a superb player that he didn't need to maintain his form in so many of the smaller tournaments. He was a law unto himself.

On the other hand, Budge probably didn't experience the pressure that the offer of a professional contract provides. Losing any one of the big tournaments could have cost me thousands of dollars. Before I met Manuel Santana at Wimbledon, Jack Kramer approached me, inquiring about my intentions and what kind of signing-on figure I would accept. Whether the discussion distracted me or whether Santana played in an inspired way I can't say. But for almost two sets it looked as though the Spaniard might win.

It was Santana who also nearly thwarted me in the French championships when he led by a set and 5-1. I recovered to beat him, and that seemed to set the pattern for every match in Paris. The gods were on my side. Martin Mulligan held a match point on me in the fourth set and Neale Fraser had two breaks in the fifth set which I ultimately won, 7-5. In the final Roy Emerson led two sets to love and was playing so well that I didn't give myself much chance. I went for my shots, hitting a little harder, and a few doubts must have crept into Roy's mind. The shots came off, and his game fell away. Roy is like that: brilliantly in command at one minute, then suddenly losing a set and struggling.

My lucky escapes in the French championships made me feel that 1962 really was my year to clean up all the major titles. But never have I been so nervous as in the United States final at Forest Hills when I played against Roy. The newspapers had done a good job in building up a tense atmosphere, and as a lot of the American players can play excellently on just one or two days I had many anxious moments on my way through. Fortunately in the final my form held. In the first two sets I concentrated so hard that tension didn't affect me. During the fourth set I got the break I wanted and started thinking of those players who snatch defeat from the jaws of victory. I became so nervous that in the last game I had difficulty holding the balls to serve. I didn't even know which side of the grip was in my palm and, consequently, on one point a volley went not toward the net but straight into the ground. Roy couldn't have realized my state, the moral being that no one ever looks as nervous as he feels. Remember that next time you get an attack of the jitters. It may help.

After achieving my Grand Slam and contributing to Australia's defense of the Davis Cup, the challenge of professional tennis held greater appeal than continuing against the same players in amateur tennis. My self-esteem was at stake. My record in the amateur game had been good, but every player at the top likes to think he can prove one day he's the best player in the world, regardless of his status. It is impossible to prove it in the amateur game today. The Wimbledon champion is not the world champion, and even achieving the Grand Slam isn't conclusive. My first year as a professional made me certain that no amateur could defeat any of the leading twelve professionals.

It is a tragedy that these professionals are unable to enrich the amateur game by playing against the still-developing amateur players. These young players are seriously handicapped in their development, because they cannot test themselves against the true champions. There seem to be, for instance, many more promising young left-handers in amateur tennis these days—players who have no doubt been encouraged by the successes of Fraser, Rose and myself and who have strong, properly formed backhands. I'm thinking particularly of Tony Roche of Australia, who has the right attitude in that he goes into every match thinking he has a chance of winning. Well, Roche may win the highest honors in the amateur game within a few years, but he is not going to develop as fully as he would playing against Hoad, Rosewall, Gimeno, MacKay, Olmedo and the rest.

Ironically, I've discovered that the professionals work much harder for the game than the players on the more glamorous amateur circuit. Of course, the game means more financially to them. But, apart from money, the professionals genuinely want to do all they can for the game that has given them security for life. I know that I am putting much more effort into the professional game than I ever put into the amateur. And one of the upshots is this chapter. I hope left-handers—and even those who have to play left-handers—will benefit.

Ken Rosewall

The Delicate Touch

Whenever I see a match in which half volleys and drop shots are much in evidence, I conclude that the players are not of a very high standard.

Some players come to rely a great deal on the half volley because they are either slow or lazy. It is normally defensive, and nobody should make a practice of advancing to the net with a defensive stroke. Moreover, on an uneven court surface the risk of being foiled by a bad bounce cannot be ignored.

As for the drop shot, which, of course, is aggressive, I feel that it loses its effectiveness when played frequently—unless an opponent is exceptionally slow. In the top company the drop shot is a rarity because all the players are fit and fast.

But both the half volley and the drop shot are essential additions to the complete player's armory and will save or win him points if used intelligently.

The half volley isn't really a volley at all, but a stroke played at the ball immediately after it bounces. As it is played at low level when the ball is moving swiftly upward, it is not always easy to control. I have heard the half volley compared to a drop kick in football, which also demands a fair degree of coordination. If mistimed, both are invariably disastrous.

If a player dawdles to the net he will find himself resorting to half volleys on or behind the service line. But the swiftest players sometimes have to play them, too, when the ball comes so quickly that they can't reach it to volley or step back to play a normal ground stroke.

Opponents like Lew Hoad and Rod Laver, with their dipping top-spin returns, force you to half-volley more than you like, and because the spin makes the ball zip off the court you are very much out on a wing and a prayer.

The professional who finds himself playing half volleys more than any of us is Pancho Segura. Watching him, you can be excused for thinking that the half volley is a fine, offensive weapon. Yet Segura only perfected his half-volleying to such an extraordinary degree because he is a little bloke lacking a big service. He knows the rest of us are going to wallop back his service, but, still, he must come into the net to have a chance.

He has the knack of keeping his half volleys low, just about at the same level as the ball comes to him, and so they're almost as good as volleys. Segura also controls their direction as though the ball were on a string. If he's caught on the forehand he usually plays a half volley across court; on the backhand he angles the ball the opposite way. And his touch is so delicate that he takes most of the pace off the ball, so that quite often it takes a bit of digging up.

The half volley has to be played in such a hurry that a player may think it's all he can do to return the ball without having any other objective. But if he merely poops the ball back against anyone fast on his feet it will be murdered. He must try to move forward as he plays his shot low into an open space and then move smartly into a better position to cut off the retort.

Don't play the half volley sloppily. You must move your feet, if there's time, so that you are sideways to the net and not too close to the ball. Remember, it is a side-arm, not an under-arm, stroke.

It is also important, if you are to exercise any control at all, to bend the knees and bring your body down, keeping your back straight. Bending the knees late in a hard match when fatigue has set in takes some doing, but the fit man will train himself to do it instinctively. Many of the half volleys that finish in the net are caused by an erect stance, resulting in the player's not getting a good look at the ball and dropping the head of his racket.

Therefore bend down until the back knee is almost touching the court, and keep the racket well up. Meet the ball in front of the body with a good, firm wrist and try to make the whole movement flow forward smoothly. The half volley played by such touch masters as Nicola Pietrangeli and Pancho Segura has the grace of a ballet movement.

If you are close to the net—and you have no right to be playing half volleys from the back of the court—you hardly need any backswing on the half volley. Power is unnecessary. What you want is placement and a ball low enough to save you from being vulnerable to a hard-hit volley or ground stroke or a lob.

If you can force a half volley in return you are doing well. Ease the ball over the net with a modified backswing and open the racket face only sufficiently for the ball to clear the tape. Those not-to-be-encouraged half volleys from the back of the court are played with a closed face and a bigger backswing if you just happen to get into trouble there.

More than on any other shot, the temptation to lift the head and see what's happening on the other side of the court is great. Resist it. Watch the ball onto the racket and don't lift the body too quickly.

Drop shots, like dink shots, can be winners if they're played perfectly and suicidal if they're not. In professional tennis most of the players are fast movers and are always looking for opportunities to force the issue from the net. Consequently, the drop shot isn't often risked. It should only be tried when your opponent is saddled on or behind the base line and you are in the forecourt. Unless the shot is timed perfectly and from fairly close range to the net, a swift opponent, who may be moving forward as you make the stroke, will get to the ball and flip it away for a winner.

The drop shot is seen more frequently in women's tennis and here it is tactically sound. Women are slower than men. They are slower off the mark, slower in changing direction and slower in running flat out. What's more, many of them only voluntarily go to the net when it's time to shake their opponent's hand. What can be more effective than to draw them forward with drop shots into the territory where they lack confidence? Maria Gueno uses this ploy as well as anyone. She can mask the shot deceptively, and this is essential when it is played so regularly.

There is no reason, of course, why a man shouldn't play drop shots more often if his opponent shows a reluctance to leave the base line. They may break up the rhythm of his game. Or if he isn't young or fully fit, they may help to tire him. These are circumstances that don't arise in professional tennis but they undoubtedly do at lower standards of the game.

John Bromwich, a supreme master of touch shots, could, when past his prime, confound many a younger, stronger player by judicious use of the drop shot. In fact, some of the officials in the New South Wales Lawn Tennis Association delighted in pitting a promising young player, who looked as if he were developing a swelled head, against the obliging Sydney veteran. After a set or so the youngster was confused by "Brom's" soft, deceptive ground strokes. He would try to steady himself by rallying from the base line. "Brom" brought him in with a drop shot. Then he tossed the ball over the flustered youngster's head.

Soon the kid didn't know whether he was coming or going—wrong-footed on the base line, surrying to the net, then frantically chasing back to reach a lob. . . . At the end of the match it was invariably the younger man who was looking for somewhere to lie down.

There used to be a feeling that in some circumstances drop shots are unsporting. I don't agree. If a player goes onto the court with a physical handicap he can't expect his opponent not to exploit it in every possible and legitimate way.

Everyone knows, for instance, that Neale Fraser has trouble

Never play a drop shot from rear court. Here, Maria Bueno, the best drop shot player among the women, executes one from perfect position. Her opponent will have a long way to go to get it.

with his legs and that they are very suspect in a long, hard match. A few years ago, after building up a big lead, Fraser lost the final of the Australian singles championship against Rod Laver in Brisbane because his legs gave out on him. Against a lesser opponent than Laver—someone without any drop shots in his bag —Fraser might have been able to see out the match from the base line, putting everything into his service. Sprinting to the net and then pulling up sharply, as Rod made him do, was the last thing he wanted.

It is obviously smart, also, to use the drop shot against somebody suffering cramp or prone to it. If he looks as though he's feeling a few twinges, why be kind to him? You have reduced him to this condition by making him run, so the logical thing is not to allow him to recover. Make him run some more.

Most of us have our favorite side on which we prefer to play the drop shot. Mine, naturally, is the backhand. The drop shot requires 100 per cent touch and I have much more touch on the backhand side.

When do I play the shot? It depends on the state of the game, the position of my opponent and the type of ball he has hit. I don't play the shot if the game is tight or if I have a chance of a breakthrough; the risk doesn't warrant it. My opponent has to be at the back of the court and if I can wrong-foot him, so much the better.

I prefer him to have played a fairly fast shot to my backhand. As I wait for the ball, the throat of the racket is cradled in my left hand, relieving some of the strain from my right. I take the ball on the rise. My wrist is firm, but the racket "dead." The face of the racket is slightly open, and at the last moment I slide it downward in a quick little motion to impart under-spin.

Giving the ball enough under-spin and yet allowing it to move forward over the net is a matter of judgment. It should barely clear the tape (careful you don't strain yourself riding it over!) and then it should "die."

It helps to deceive your opponent if your backswing and general approach to the shot is the same as for a drive. The decision to make it a drop shot comes in the last split-second when all the factors—the speed of the ball, the angle at which it's approaching, and your position and that of your opponent—crystallize in your mind.

If the ball doesn't "sit up" after it has cleared the net—and on grass, at any rate, a ball with under-spin on it won't—your opponent may have difficulty in getting to it without fouling the net. He may try a delicate counter-drop shot or flick up a lob. The chances of either being very effective are not great. On the other hand, if you've goofed and he reaches the ball comfortably he will probably be able to whip it past you.

Off my backhand, I prefer to play a drop shot to my opponent's forehand side. I don't like giving such secrets away, because it could cost me money, but I guess most of the professional boys know about this particular predilection anyway. The point is that most players say it is safer to angle drop shots instead of playing them straight ahead. Maybe they're right. It's just that I feel happier doing it my way.

Pancho Segura

Competitiveness

When I was a kid of about seven in Ecuador one of the members of the swanky tennis club where my father was caretaker tossed me an unwanted racket. It was much too heavy for my skinny little arms. I recall that I was the smallest, sickest, most rickety-legged kid in the district. Malaria and a couple of hernias knocked the stuffing out of me, and at my lowest ebb a crutch would have been a more practical gift than a tennis racket.

Now, being physically weak was certainly a disadvantage when I started using that first unwieldy racket, but such a handicap made it necessary to develop my cunning. I had to think hard about the game if the bigger kids weren't going to trample all over me. And I have been thinking hard about it ever since.

Sometimes I have looked over the net and seen a long-armed monster such as Gonzales or Trabert or McGregor on the other side and I've groaned. "My God, Pancho," I've said, "there ought to be a law against this."

I like to think that mostly it's my strategy that's saved me, or at any rate made the other fellow know he's been in a match. This strategy has been built up over thirty years against all types of opposition. Harnessed to it is a mighty keen competitiveness. I know how to exploit any situation that occurs on a tennis court. Any fellow who allows me an inch will find me taking a mile; I don't care who he is. Even though now I'm in my forties, if anyone sets up a faulty pattern of play on any point he is bound to lose it.

Before I come to what are the correct and faulty patterns of play let's go over a few fundamentals.

First, the importance of defense. Every player should try to develop a defensive game because it will provide him with something in reserve. If he can lob from both sides of the court he will be ready for emergencies.

A good golfer, a Palmer or a Snead, occasionally gets into as dire trouble as any weekend duffer. But the difference is in his ability to play a recovery shot. He has practiced that shot over and over again for just such an emergency. The tennis player should give equal attention to developing his own recovery shots.

Maybe he's returned service badly and is running from the middle of the court to pick up an angled volley. The only way he can give himself time to get back to the middle is by playing a high lob as opposed to an offensive passing shot.

He is not, you see, in an offensive position. Anyone who runs from the middle and leaves one side of the court open is in a defensive position. And for him the lob is the smart shot to play, even against a deadly smasher, because the lob will raise serious doubts in the opponent's mind about advancing too close to the net.

By lobbing a few times, if only as a variation, a player makes certain that he has enough room to make a passing shot at other times. The rash and the reckless try to pass all the time. They should heed Pancho's advice: The number of attempted passing shots that get through in a top-class match is very low.

Also defensive are the delicate angled shots from both wings. They may be played when there is room across court. The opponent expects a drive or a lob. Instead, he's unbalanced and shifted from the middle by an angled shot. He covers it only at the expense of leaving space to which the next shot can be hit freely.

The value in possessing a reliable defensive lob and defensive angled shots, as well as a strong drive, is that they create uncertainty in the mind of the opponent.

This is something for which you must always strive, no matter what your grade of tennis. How often do experienced players beat strong, tear-away opponents, simply by denying them the chance to settle into their normal, stereotyped game!

Mixing up lobs, defensive angled shots and drives will knock the opponent's confidence. He will never be sure which of the three he will have to cope with.

But bear in mind that the angles must be made from inside the base line after the opponent has made his first or second volley. An angled shot from on or behind the base line doesn't pay. Because the ball has farther to travel, it is not as deceptive. If the opponent reaches it he will either slam it for a winner or hit it short. And from the base line it will take some running down.

I play my angled shots when my opponent least expects them, because, as I say, even in defense the element of surprise mustn't be overlooked. An angle carries greater risk than a lob, and I don't usually resort to one at 30-all or 30-40, as I am conscious that if it doesn't come off I stand to lose the game.

It is important *always* to know the score. Knowing the score and my opponent's weaknesses, keeping my eye on the ball and concentrating so that I'm oblivious to whether I'm in Quito or Quebec are big factors in my game.

Discovering an opponent's weaknesses is basic to tennis strategy, yet it's amazing how many players are haphazard in this essential. Everyone has a weakness unless he's a Rosewall or a Gonzales, and even they don't hit some shots as well as others.

When I'm playing somebody for the first time I quickly realize which of my shots make him most uncomfortable. It takes me one set at the most. I serve to both sides and judge from the weight of the returns the relative strength of his forehand and backhand ground strokes. When he serves and comes to the net I throw a few soft balls at him, or fast ones, to see how he handles speed and where he tends to place his volleys. I toss the ball up high to assess his overhead and how he maneuvers himself.

Say I'm playing a fellow with a game like Rosewall's. It's soon obvious that his forehand is his weaker shot, so I must concentrate on his forehand as much as possible. Occasionally I swing to his backhand, but only when I have him on the run. Though it's his best shot, he's playing it when the odds are against him. This all helps to undermine his confidence.

To this kind of player—one with a weaker forehand—I will hit high, soft balls to the forehand. He will have to generate pace from his weaker side, and to do this he must try to stroke the ball and control it, which perhaps is difficult for him. A fast, low ball he may block. He may maintain pace by keeping his racket firm. But a slow, high ball will put his weaker stroke under pressure.

Assuming that a player has appraised his opponent's game accurately, he must incorporate that knowledge in the over-all framework of percentage tennis.

The vital points are from 30-15 on—30-all, 30-40, deuce, etc. Nobody can hope to become a champion in the top league unless he knows how to play them. One of the fascinating aspects of tennis is that a player can make the most placements and win the most games yet still lose the match. It follows that the key points demand a greater effort. On these, above all, a player must attack his opponent's weaknesses.

A really significant point is at 30-15. It can open up a two-points lead, and once any moderately good player has reached 40-15 he wins the game seven times out of ten.

Let's imagine I have 30-15 on my opponent's service. If he serves his first ball into court I'm not going to be too aggressive, because the ball will be moving fast and he'll be coming into the net. I believe in being aggressive only when I have time. Taking a full backswing against a fast service is asking for trouble. My aim will be to try to keep the ball low, hitting it down the middle or to his weakness. In this way I'll get to play on his volley, and that's what I want. If, however, his first service fails, I will attack his second service, moving in behind my shot, hoping to cut off his reply and make him press. Maybe as he sees me moving in he'll double-fault.

If I hold 40-15 on my opponent's service I will be even more aggressive. On this score, but only on this score (except, of course on 40-love) is a gamble justified.

On the other hand, being down 15-30 or 15-40 calls for conservative tennis. Most likely the service will come to the backhand. The best play is to return the ball across court to the backhand as here the maximum amount of court space is available. Provided the opponent is smart, he'll hit it back across court again, and so once more I live. I get to play another shot. If he tries to make a shot down the line he's taking a big risk unless my return is high. As a rule, therefore, return low across court and always make your opponent earn these vital points.

Now let's assume that I'm down 15-30 on my own service. I'll make sure my service is in and serve right at the opponent. Right at his solar plexus, so that he won't be able to angle his return. In fact, he'll have to move pretty slickly to return the ball at all and I should have a comfortable volley.

Never, if I can help it, will I allow my opponent to attack me when I'm down. Lacking a powerful cannonball service, it's important that my first service go in and be well placed, because in a tight spot this is the stroke that counts.

I can't emphasize too strongly the need to adapt tactics to the score. For instance, never make a drop shot or stop volley at 15-30 or 30-40; if it doesn't win the point you're in bad trouble.

Similarly, it depends on the state of the game whether an attempt should be made for an outright winner with a smash. On a key point smash the ball hard, but don't aim for the lines. Be satisfied in moving the opponent away from the middle, for then he has lost command of the point.

These days all the young fellows try to develop the serve-volley game, and anybody with ambition must learn not only how to volley efficiently but how to counter the outstanding volleyer. Sometimes a guy has a great service as well as a great volley. Here is a champion—a Gonzales. The only hope is to lob in an attempt to reduce the number of his volleys. In addition, he must be crowded on his second service in an effort to make him rush his first volley.

There are two types of great volleyers—the fellows who can make a brilliant, probing volley from about the service line on

The return of Pancho Segura's serve has been made low to his backhand and has caught him in a difficult position on the service line. Pancho has had to dive across and make a backhand half-volley. As he measures the flight of the oncoming ball, he supports his racket with his left hand and makes his move to position with a long right-foot stride. There is hardly any backswing as Segura gets right down over his planted right foot, with his left foot dragging as a brake. His free arm helps his balance. In this sequence the ball isn't visible—it has hit the court and been half-volleyed between frames 3 and 4—but it is evident that Segura has hit it with a slightly open racket face. From so low a position at such close quarters to the net, he had to do so.

their way to the net, and the others whose second volley, when they've reached the net, is devastating. I prefer to play those in the second category. At least, as they advance, I get a chance to lob. But the first type can shut their man right out of the game.

Kramer, for example, was tough because he punched his first volley across court with such pace that his opponent finished in the alleys. He allowed no answer.

Gonzales is different. His volley doesn't match Kramer's but his service is so dynamic that frequently he is volleying weak returns.

One of the most spectacular volleyers is Hoad. He will hit fantastic volleys off difficult balls and in top form he'll beat his man badly. Luckily for the rest of us, he also misses easy shots. He is the kind of player who always gives his opponent a chance. None of the professionals beats himself more than Lew. As an amateur he lacked patience and concentration and abused his magnificent power. As a professional he has matured, but he still tends to try to win a point in one shot instead of employing all the court with two or three more conservative shots.

Against these great volleyers you are giving yourself some protection if you play down the middle, because no matter how brilliant he is, a volleyer finds it hard to produce an angle from the middle of the court. What he likes is a ball which he has to reach sideways.

Think back on some of the great matches you've seen and you'll recall that all the spectacular volleys were made when the player had to reach wide for them—Sedgman leaping to his forehand, or Trabert flinging himself onto a backhand.

Anyone who slaps a forehand return across court on the 15-love point against a good volleyer faces the risk of the ball's being angled away with a forehand volley. A great volleyer may even volley it straight down the line. But return the ball down the middle and you'll get to play another shot. Maybe then you can go for a passing shot or a lob or an angle.

What I'm trying to stress is that your opponent must be made to earn the point. Don't feed his volley. Don't throw the point away. Tennis is won more on unnecessary errors than on forced errors.

Sometimes when I'm serving I deliberately stay on the base

line until after my opponent has returned the ball. This is a gimmick to break the rhythm of his game when he's expecting me automatically to follow my service to the net. Even if the point is lost through staying back it is worthwhile. Instead of working himself into a groove chipping to my feet, he has to go for length on his return, and the good-length ball is easier to volley than the dipping shot.

In other words, I change my pace; I never let the other guy become settled. I can play from the net or the base line, because my ground strokes are sound. I can wait. . . . And perhaps he's so intense and so eager to win that he rushes into errors. When he's driving the ball really fast, yet with not much placement, I let the ball bounce and rally with him, because those fast balls are hard to volley.

My strongest shot, of course, is my double-handed forehand. It came to me naturally as a pint-sized kid in Ecuador and was one of the benefits I derived from being unable to swing the racket comfortably with one hand. The double-handed shot had my body rotating forward, leaning into the ball, and this happens to be the way all shots should be hit. Therefore, though I use both hands, the position of my racket and the motion of my body, except for an exaggerated swiveling of the shoulder, is orthodox.

I wish I had learned to play my backhand with a double-handed grip too, as John Bromwich used to do. But as a kid I was discouraged. The double-handed shot may reduce reach, but the player is closer to the ball and able to be more deceptive.

Over the years I have developed a lot of deception with my forehand. I can hit it anywhere and change the direction of the stroke at the last faction of a second.

This kind of control comes only after a player knows his potential with each kind of ball. Every ball can't be struck in the same way. A soft ball requires a full backswing to whip up pace; a fast ball needs the minimum backswing.

A little top-spin is advisable on most shots, as it brings the ball down quickly. The slice can be useful, too, especially when it's as beautifully controlled as Rosewall's. A player equipped with both shots can slice the ball when it's short and he's following it into the net, and he can apply top-spin on the passing shot.

Naturally, since I have less control on my backhand, the other professionals attack me there all the time. Whenever possible, I try to run around their second service in order to take the ball on my forehand. Now and again, as they throw the ball up, I move; at other times I merely sway my shoulders as though I'm going to move. This stratagem has been of immense value to me.

Every aspiring champion should try to make himself flexible throughout his body, and especially around his chest and shoulders. Zigzagging in a field, as a football player does, and shadow boxing are useful exercises.

What you do when you "fake" is move your shoulders and chest in an opposite direction from your feet. By pretending to shift in one direction you may bluff your opponent into rushing his service or serving where you want him to serve. And such harrying worries him, keeps him guessing. He may even double-fault. The old school of player may regard all this sort of thing as unethical, but I don't intend to give it up until they show me something in the rules prohibiting it.

While on the subject of flexibility, I must point out that anyone who tries to play tennis with an erect, rigid stance will never get anywhere—except in a modeling school. Tennis is predominantly a low-level game. So you must bend the knees and crouch. As in skiing, the body movement is controlled by the knees.

You must also be quick with your hands, shifting the racket from one side to the other as quickly as Matt Dillon draws his gun.

As well as searching for an opponent's weaknesses in stroke equipment, a player must judge his stamina, his ability to fight out a long, hard match. When satisfied that an opponent's physical condition isn't too good, make him run. Although an easy shot may be set up, don't put it away. In coming to the net make sure that he can reach your volleys, or if you stay back, try to move him around with probing drives. Then, when he's drooping, turn on the aggression.

A player's lack of fitness can usually be gauged by his reluctance to advance to the net behind his returns. Once, playing an unfit Frank Kovacs, who had a very dangerous return of service, I remained on the base line to trade shots with him until the venom in that return was gone. He was so much easier to beat them.

Often, especially in old fellows like me, it's necessary to conserve one's energy. Supposing the match has dragged on into the fifth set and one lucky break is going to determine it. The sensible attitude is to go flat out to win the first two points on the opponent's service. If you win them or share them, by all means maintain the pressure for the whole game. But if you lose them, save strength for your next service.

By using brains and experience, older players can go a long way toward covering deficiencies in stamina. A lot of rubbish is spoken by people who think that because players have reached a certain age they must be on the decline. As I said at the start, I was a weak kid and it wasn't until I was thirty, when I had turned professional and was doing building-up exercises, that I became really strong.

Right through my thirties I was in top physical condition; in my forties I still hold my own. At thirty-six I won a big tournament on grass in Sydney, beating Sedgman in four sets and Gonzales 13-11 in the fifth. A year later I won a Round Robin in California, beating every other competitor, including Rosewall in the final. By pacing myself and knowing how to play the vital points, I have compensated for my reduced pace and strength.

Tennis invariably is influenced by outside factors—the sun, the wind, the condition of the court. I size them up the moment I step on to the court and use them to my advantage. I lob into a wind, never when it's behind me. And if the sun is dazzling or there are blinding electric lights suspended above an indoor court it suits my lobbing perfectly. No one likes looking for a ball against a bright light.

I never try to annoy my opponent, but if he annoys me I will certainly retaliate—by stalling, by questioning line calls, or by acting in any other irritating way.

My weakest shot has always been my second service, just as it is Rosewall's. We are both small men and we cannot attack with our second ball. My vulnerability here is a greater hazard now because of my age. Tall guys like Gonzales, Trabert and Gimeno can move into my second service and hit down on me. So I try to place my first service, rather than attempt an ace, and trust errors rarely occur.

But, on the whole, surviving into middle age as a top-class player is a matter of having the correct mental attitude. If anyone says, "Heck, I can't expect to be able to do this at my age," he hasn't got a chance of doing it. Gardnar Mulloy is about six years older than me, yet by looking after his physical condition and playing intelligently he still manages to win matches in the major amateur championships. And look at Archie Moore and Sugar Ray Robinson fighting late into their forties. How did they do it? By taking care of themselves and punching wisely. As for me, the edge may have gone from my power, but I can lob and hit angles better than I could twenty years ago.

Like most of the other professionals, I keep two or three rackets by me not too tightly strung, because in our class of tennis control is more important than power. All players must appreciate as they grow older that they have to rely increasingly on touch.

And they can't afford long lay-offs. It makes me shudder to think what happens when I don't play for two or three weeks. In my first match back one of the youngsters grabs me and beats my brains out. It is only by superior strategy, and because I need the money, that I'm able to rehabilitate myself.

Lew Hoad

Lobs—and How to Beat Them

There hasn't been a better example of the value of a good lob than in the semifinals of the 1962 Wembley championships when the perennial Pancho Segura looked to have Ken Rosewall on toast. Segura was in fine enough form to beat anyone in the world, and in the fifth set, when he led 4-3 with his service to follow, we all thought it was curtains for "Muscles." They are both tremendous lobbers, but not one ball had been tossed in the air by Rosewall for two or three sets—simply because it hadn't been needed. Now, Segura, anxious to hold his service for 5-3, bounded injudiciously close to the net, something he rarely does. Rosewall saw him out of the corner of his eye. He lobbed three successive times, the ball each time landing within inches of the base line. Segura got to two of the lobs, but at that stage the effort was just too much for him. He dropped his service—and his bundle. At the crux of the match Rosewall had broken his heart.

I remember a similar situation playing Mervyn Rose in the

Australian championships at Brisbane when he grabbed a dangerous lead over me and was playing so confidently that he seemed sure of victory. I was on the ropes floundering as Rose set himself for the kill. He was like a deadly cat at the net until a couple of desperate lobs that sailed over his head raised the base-line chalk. Both balls he reckoned would fall out, but they didn't. In the tension and the heat, his confidence seeped away and I went on to win.

The point about this kind of lobbing is that it must be disguised, for if the stroke is telegraphed it loses effect. Most of the great lobbers, such as Rosewall and Segura, prepare for the lob as though making a drive. Until they open the face of the racket at the last fraction of a second the trajectory of the ball is hard to anticipate. They don't shorten their actions. Their rackets merely start a little lower and they follow through upwards.

Young players, and good ones at that, tend to despise the lob as a refuge for mediocrities. They belt away at their passing shots even when they are forced way out of court and their opponent is encamped at the net.

How many times in an amateur championship have you seen a youngster just manage to reach a deep, wide ball and attempt to slam it ferociously past his opponent? Invariably, the ball hits the net or lands out of court or is picked off.

Amateurs, who otherwise are brilliant stroke-makers, such as Dennis Ralston and Bob Hewitt, seem to give little consideration to the lob. It is not fitting that I should take them to task too severely, because in my own early days I was a reluctant lobber myself. Willingness to lob and the judgment required in knowing when to lob comes only with maturity, I guess. It is certainly a fact that the professionals, who've had twice the experience of the amateurs in their early twenties, use the lob infinitely more.

The toughest lobber in the amateur game I ever came up against was John Bromwich, whose control was absolutely uncanny. Bromwich liked a breeze that he could exploit against a net-rusher. He lofted the ball so accurately in the wind that you'd swear he had some sort of wind gauge and computer in his pocket.

Lobs fall into two categories—offensive and defensive. The

offensive lob is usually made when the opponent has stationed himself close to the net and the ball is low and short. A player ought to be able to sense where his opponent will be from the shot he has hit, and so, making up his mind quickly, he essays an offensive lob. The racket face strikes the ball flat from slightly underneath, floating it just out of the opponent's reach and allowing it to fall close to the base line.

If you can imagine a four-iron golf shot you have the picture of an offensive lob.

The whole movement requires as much touch and precision as the passing shot, perhaps even more. It is extremely difficult to bring off, but it must be attempted if the opponent is fleet-footed and is racing to within a few feet of the net, because it will keep him in two minds.

A succession of attempted passing shots will help the net-rusher to get in a volleying groove unless they are interspersed with a few offensive lobs. If the lob is masked he will have little chance of pulling up, retracing his steps and retrieving it. And even if he does, you have command of the point.

A few players, notably Vic Seixas, have tried to develop a top-spin lob. Seixas relied almost exclusively on a top-spin drive, and as he used the same action for the lob, it was hard to detect and even harder to smash because the ball dipped sharply with the spin. I estimate, however, that Seixas averaged only about one in twenty of the top-spin lobs he tried; it was such a tough shot for him to control.

My advice is to forget about spin in lobbing. Although I have a heavily top-spun drive, I never use a top-spin lob. Maybe I come over the ball, but I don't consciously try to spin it as Seixas did. I realize that hitting up and over the ball with top-spin can be devastating if the ball lands close to the base line, because the opponent has no chance of running down the ball as it bites into the court and bounds past the base line. On the other hand, percentage-wise the attempt isn't worth it.

The safest offensive lob is played with a firm wrist, the racket being under the ball, which sends it fairly fast on a low enough trajectory to catch the opponent off-balance. If he is right-handed he is likely to be most vulnerable over his left shoulder, so when it's practicable aim there.

In a long, grueling match such lobs are tactically sound. They help to tire the other fellow out, even if he's sharp enough to jump up and smash them. Obviously, if he's weak overhead you must play them for their outright winning potential as well as their long-term tactical value.

The defensive lob is employed when a player is completely out of position and only manages to get his racket to the ball. It could be that he is so far out of court and stretched out so awkwardly that anything else but a lob would be suicidal. Therefore he tosses the ball high into the air to give him sufficient time to recover.

A ball that is lobbed within three feet of the base line while the player is on the run and out of position is as good as anyone can hope for. Nine times out of ten the opponent will fall back, wait for the ball to bounce and then smash. In the meantime, the player who has lobbed will have scurried back into a stronger position. He has been worked into a desperate spot, he's been smart enough to give himself a respite, and though he still isn't out of trouble, he has a chance of returning the smash and virtually starting the point all over again.

Control of the lob comes only with practice; it's not a bad idea to get someone hitting balls hard and wide to your forehand and backhand so that you're forced to run hard and scoop them up.

As in the offensive lob, a misjudged ball that falls short is a sitter to be smashed away. Perseverance in perfecting your lobbing touch will always pay off.

As for the direction of the lob, the ball hit diagonally gives you five or six feet more court, and so, diagonally, you can hit a little harder and higher.

Though I'm not far off thirty, I am still learning how to play lawn tennis better, and one of my most important lessons has been in lobbing. Playing with fellows like Segura, who has lobbing down to a fine art, has been an education in itself. Even today, whenever I'm at the net against Segura, I'm never sure when he will toss the ball over my head. And this is how he drags strong young fellows down to his pace.

At Wembley in 1962 I played Earl Buchholz. In five sets he didn't lob once. In spite of the length of the match I wasn't really tired at the end. But if I had played Segura he would have thrown up at least one or two lobs every game and possibly three or four in one rally. In the fifth set I might have been a cot case.

Playing against a strong lobber, you find yourself running from the net to perhaps eight feet behind the base line to make a shot, and then moving off quickly as your return is intercepted at the net. If your opponent, in turn, has committed himself strongly to a net position, it may be your turn to lob, and his to run back. This kind of rally can be more exacting than any other. It makes a wonderful and exciting spectacle—as the gasps from our galleries have often testified.

Conditions must always be taken into account in lobbing. It is easier to control a lob hitting into the wind rather than with it, and if the sun is particularly bad from one end it is only sensible to take advantage of the fact and lob into it.

Nobody knows all these tricks better than Segura. At Wembley, for instance, he lobs up the middle of the court all the time, because that's where the lights are hanging. Once the ball is under the lights you lose track of it. He won't lob on either side of the court out of the lights or diagonally so that the ball is only temporarily lost, the villain. Of course, there is nothing to prevent us from dishing out the same treatment to Segura.

There are several players who are so deadly overhead that if you are at all loose in lobbing it is "goodnight nurse." Pancho Gonzales is tall and agile and allows very few balls to pass over his head. Tony Trabert is another tall, powerful man who really lays into his smashes, while Rosewall is fantastically accurate even when the lob is deep.

Which brings me to the answer to the lob—the smash. Anybody who aspires to play the serve-volley game must be able to kill the ball with his overhead smash. Unless he possesses this ability, he will lack real confidence at the net. A perceptive opponent will lob him until he has a stiff neck looking up at the sky.

I cannot imagine how any player can go boldly into the net to volley, if at the back of his mind there lurks a fear of being embarrassed by the ball overhead.

Conversely, nothing characterizes the class player more than his smashing. When he leaps into the air in mid-court to crash a ball obliquely away for a winner he looks a champion—and the odds are that he feels one, too. For a cleanly hit smash is more satisfying and morale-building than any other stroke, and nothing is so discouraging to an opponent early in a match than to have his lobs severely punished.

But the beginner finds it depressingly difficult to judge a smash. He always waits for the ball to bounce and pushes it back weakly or else smashes it wildly into the back-stopping. He may even run right back and play a ground stroke. I can only say that until he masters the smash and becomes confident of putting the overhead balls away he will never get very far.

The smash, the most spectacular shot in the game, is not played nearly as often as ground strokes, and yet because it is so vital in the modern game there is a good case to be made for it to be practiced even more. Hitting a ball overhead with power while moving backward is something that few players can do instinctively when they take up the game. But by working hard on the shot it should be possible for any reasonably coordinated person to knock off the shorter lobs, at any rate, with a fair degree of rhythm.

The first essential in smashing is to keep the body side-on to the net throughout the stroke. If the ball is short and has to be approached, most of the leading players go toward it with a sort of sideways skip that takes them nicely into position under the ball.

But if a pretty good offensive lob has to be countered it means moving backward quickly and jumping high enough to make contact.

The ideal place to strike the ball is when it's about a foot in front of the head over the right eye. Jumping gives you more chance of hitting down, and as you go up, springing off your right foot with your left foot flung forward in the air, you use your left arm for balance and lining up the ball.

Don't be inhibited in your leap or in steadying yourself with the free arm. Try smashing a ball with the left arm behind the back and you will see what an important part it plays in the stroke.

The arm is straight at impact as the wrist snaps down over the top of the ball, imparting power and direction. As the racket comes through, the body ought to jackknife into the shot. Stiffness is a handicap and the more flexible your body the better smasher you are going to be.

It is also vital that the ball be watched in its entire flight until struck.

A sideways stance enables the ball to be hit across court, down the center or out to the opponent's backhand side. Most right-handed players, when "going for the doctor," tend to favor hitting the ball away from them: that is, to the backhand of a right-handed opponent. It is more difficult to smash to the forehand, but if, as you are about to smash, you realize your opponent has the backhand covered you can flick your wrist and hit a type of sliced smash down to the forehand. I find myself doing this quite a lot. Although the shot lacks power, the other fellow has to run from the backhand to the forehand side, by which time you are on top of the net ready for his next shot—if he can make it.

Angling the smash can be important, more so in doubles than in singles. A good, deep smash to either corner will usually suffice in singles to win the point, because the ball has too much pace for the opponent to control even if he gets his racket to it. Mostly he's standing behind the base line waiting for the smash and, if the ball is deep, it is past him in a flash. The chances of his making a passing shot if he gets onto the ball are remote. Unless the fellow takes a real gamble he will have to give you another high deep lob. Then it's best to let the ball bounce, giving yourself more time to fix it properly in your sights and wham it for a winner.

When to jump and when to wait for the ball to bounce are questions that are answered with personal experience. Broadly, I'd say that if your opponent has played an offensive lob you have no choice; you must jump and give it a good whack.

You are not losing the initiative, however, if you let a high defensive lob land, especially if it is deep into a corner. It is falling almost perpendicularly. It may go out. And anyway you are putting pressure on yourself by trying to take it while moving backward. I'm sure it's better to give yourself time to get behind the flight of the ball. If you're experienced you'll have a fair idea from the height of the lob how high the ball will bounce and you'll be all set to give it the works.

Moving backward to take his opponent's lob, Lew Hoad keeps his side to the net while jockeying into a solid position from which he can spring for the smash. Eyes riveted on the ball throughout its flight, he gets his lift at the critical moment of timing with a jump off the right foot, meeting the ball (frame 9) in front of the head, so that he can hit down on it. Wrist snap and the maintenance of balance with the left arm are essential to a powerful smash, and the wrist is the factor which can vary its direction as well.

Some coaches advocate an elaborate wind-up for the smash. I'm all against it. In this respect, and also in that sometimes both feet are off the ground, the smash is different from the service. A powerful service demands a full, flourishing wind-up, but remember the server throws the ball up himself and it has no horizontal movement at all. A big wind-up prior to smashing only increases your margin for error and it is more advisable to have the racket held high poised for a shorter, chopper-like blow at the ball.

Ashley Cooper and Barry MacKay are examples of players who take too big a swing at a smash with the result that the ball is as likely to be buried in the net as to go over it. Smashing calls for split-second timing, and Cooper and MacKay don't help themselves to achieve it by their big swings. In contrast, Rosewall's racket travels a very short distance when he smashes. Although he is not a big man, his timing, accuracy and consistency make him a formidable smasher.

One of the best smashers the world has seen in the last ten to fifteen years was Mervyn Rose. He had a very short wind-up and could jump like a kangaroo. At his peak he used to fly two and a half feet off the ground while traveling backward and still maintain perfect balance. He was also very deceptive. A left-hander, he could slice the ball away to his opponent's backhand or smash it to his forehand without disclosing his intentions. It was Rose's smashing that was such a large factor in his success as a doubles player, because he angled the ball so well.

Smashes needn't be hit so hard and flat and deep in doubles. They are usually better angled or aimed at the opponent's feet, and Rose was a master of these tactics.

Is it necessary to smash with every ounce of energy, to give each overhead everything you've got? Rosewall proves that it isn't every time he goes onto the court.

I am a much more vigorous smasher than Rosewall, but I don't smash as hard as in my amateur days for the simple reason that if I give the ball a whack seven or eight times in a match my troublesome back lays me low the following day. So I've concentrated on placement. My smashing is all the better for it.

Smashing is strenuous. It imposes a severe strain on the stomach and shoulder muscles as well as the back, and these days I don't like to stretch full out on a smash until I'm properly warmed up.

Systematic strengthening of the muscles that have to carry the load should be carried out if you're aiming to break into top-class tennis. And keep on practicing until you know you can put away a ball from any position on the court, not overlooking those "sitters" that fall in the forecourt. Those are the balls that the professionals *never* miss.

Tony Trabert
The Strategy of Doubles

Look at any of the greatest doubles combinations the world has known and you'll find they had one thing in common: they all eliminated guesswork. For Borotra and Brugnon, Tilden and Richards, Bromwich and Quist every move had a meaning. They played according to well-tested principles. And because they played together over many years they had confidence in each other's responses to any situation.

Today we professionals take a more analytical approach to doubles than any group of players before us. The volleying exchanges that draw gasps from the crowds are not due merely to sharp reflexes and athleticism, but to deep understanding of the game by both pairs. Each man knows from the kind of shot an opponent hits what his partner is going to do, and, consequently, he covers all the possibilities on his side of the court.

We did our groundwork as amateurs, picking up every title

the game has to offer and a lot of silver mugs besides. As professionals our know-how helps us to put a few more bucks in the bank.

The guy who taught me doubles was Billy Talbert, who's devoted as much thought to tennis as anyone these last couple of decades. Talbert started to help me when I was twelve. When I was nineteen he took me on a European tour in which we won every doubles tournament we entered. The only tournament in which we didn't play together was Wimbledon. I paired with Budge Patty and we made history in the quarter-finals when we defeated Frank Sedgman and Ken McGregor, 6-4, 31-29, 7-9, 6-2. The second set was the longest in history and caused Wimbledon to change one of its rules. Up till then the balls were changed not after a specific number of games, but at the end of each set.

It had drizzled a few times while we were playing—it often does in England—and at 20-all the balls were very heavy. When the umpire refused us permission to use new balls I got mad and said, "What are we going to do if I knock all these six balls out of the stadium—stand here for the rest of the afternoon?" And so, by raising Cain, we negotiated a compromise. We were given back the balls that had been used for ten games in the first set!

My other doubles matches on that first European tour were less controversial and considerably shorter. I played in the ad court, and I've stuck to that spot ever since.

When it came to controlling the play, Talbert was without peer. He kept the ball low, though he didn't always hit it hard, and he did all the probing.

I was the bludgeon. I waited until my partner had set the ball up for me, then moved in and put it away. The crowds cheered me more than Billy, except the knowing ones who appreciated that it was my partner who set up the openings.

The only other amateur I partnered consistently was Vic Seixas, with whom I won the United States, Australian and French doubles titles. Seixas had some pretty fair weapons—a strong service, volley and smash. He also had a few specialties, such as a top-spin offensive lob, that were annoying and difficult for opponents. Initially, his tactics weren't the best, but as we developed he learned rapidly such things as how not to open up our court with his shots.

As a professional, I've played with three outstanding right-court players (anyone who gets stuck with me in doubles *has* to play the right court). There isn't a player in the world who wouldn't jump at the chance of having Lew Hoad as a partner; and Frank Sedgman, a great all-around champion, was another tremendous partner.

But it was Rex Hartwig's right-court play which I admired most. He was so versatile. He took the ball very early, either slicing his backhand return, or hitting it flat, or slicing the ball softly so that it dropped like a feather. His backhand return was so good that he could bang the ball served down the center back into the server's alley. The ball traveled fast and was angled enough to force the server out of court, and unless he somehow made a great volley, the man at the net moved across and intercepted to win the point. "Wrecker" was equally deadly with his forehand. He took the ball early there, too, and could hit it through the center or roll it with top-spin at the server's feet.

Now if you can hit shots like that—and if you can, come and see us; we may make you an offer—the only way you can fail as a doubles player is in not capitalizing on your ability because of poor knowledge of doubles strategy. And it is mostly strategy with which I will concern myself in this chapter.

The whole basis of good doubles play is in trying to hit your shots—returns of service, volleys and everything else—low into the opponents' court. When the ball is below the net, they must hit up. You will then have achieved your initial objective, which is to be in a position to hit down on your opponents.

Let's look at the role of the server. He must try to get his first service into play as often as possible. By that, I don't mean he should content himself with easy spin serves, because a competent team will move in on them, return the ball low and seize the initiative. No, the server must strive to serve a ball that is well placed and lands deep, a ball maybe of three-quarter pace. He must come in behind that service and always, I repeat *always*, be inside the service line when he makes his first volley.

He volleys down to the feet of the player who's returned service, assuming that this man has followed in his return as a good player tries to do. The ball is high? Then an outright winner must be attempted by volleying hard at the nearest man, the stationary man at the net.

If the ball is low, or at any rate not high enough to attempt an outright winner, the volleyer should try to extract some of its speed and volley it back down at the feet of the incoming player.

Some players make the mistake of shooting for the obvious opening, say through the center of the court. This is often a trap, for both opponents, if they are seasoned, will cover that ball by instinct and reflex.

Here I will let you in on one of the secrets that has served me well. When I have a volley or a short ball bouncing inside the service line that I want to ram at my opponent I don't hit haphazardly at any part of him. I aim at the right hip—provided he's a right-handed player. Most guys in the ready position hold their racket angled from right to left. It's the natural way to point the racket. They can cover a ball coming to their left side, but a quick ball to their right hip or right side will trap them. They can't get their racket into that position fast enough.

Placement of the service is most important in top-flight competition. Although most players have a weakness, which must be exploited whenever possible, it normally pays when serving in the first court to serve to the backhand—that is, up the center. Why? Because the receiver is deprived of any great angle on his return. He has three alternatives: he can pull his backhand back toward the net man or down his alley, which can only succeed once in a while because the net man is alert, waiting; he can return up through the center; or he can try to chip the ball wide of the server's forehand, a soft delicate shot that is supposed to fall at the server's feet. The odds are that he won't be too successful, whichever of these shots he plays.

But what happens if the server sends the ball wide to the forehand? For a start, he commits the cardinal doubles sin of opening up his court—a disaster on which I will elaborate later. The opponent can try to shoot a forehand up the alley. This is a distinct possibility which the net man must guard against by moving to his left.

A good player receiving the ball on his forehand knows what the net man must do, so he feels free to take more liberties on the shot through the center. A ball that the net man might normally cut off eludes him because he is leaning the other way. The receiver is also presented with a possible angle. If he has a strong cross-court forehand he may be able to hit an outright winner. Generally, then, the server must serve up the center (if his opponent is right-handed), varying this tactic only rarely as a surprise, or directly at the receiver, forcing him to play a shot while trying at the same time to get his body out of the way.

Serving to the second court, it may be said that the ball up the center line again is the one that eliminates the angle. But left-court players of any merit usually can take that ball very early, enabling them to get into a volleying position almost as quickly as the server. It is safer to serve deep to the backhand corner, because then the receiver has to move to his left out of court to make the return. He is not gaining the advantage of any movement toward the net as he would on the forehand. In fact, with his right foot across, his weight is going the other way, making it practically impossible for him to follow his return into the net effectively.

A very sound ploy whether serving, volleying or returning service is to hit the ball straight at the opponent. As I have said, he has to worry not only about the ball but also about shifting his body out of the way.

A slice serve that moves into the receiver can be extremely effective. Every service, of course, ought to be deep. And remember that though you vary direction according to the weaknesses of the opponents, it is normally least dangerous to attack the backhand.

The man at the net has a very important part to play in enabling his partner to hold his service, even though he may not touch the ball. He must loom as a constant threat, intercepting a lot of balls without moving too far and opening gaps. Much depends naturally on the quality of the serving. Strong serving will produce high or weak returns that the net man can pick off without strain.

The way he can really help his partner is by faking and feinting. Say that I'm at the net. I know my partner basically is going to serve down the center in the deuce court and wide to the backhand in the ad court. As the ball crosses the net, I'll give a

Whether on the backhand side (ABOVE) or the forehand (BELOW), you must get your body down to make a low volley. Tony Trabert shows how it's done, with his trailing knee in both cases only inches above the ground. In the case of the forehand shot, he's managed to do it despite the fact that he's had to hustle even to get far enough up in the forecourt to make the shot.

very early fake, a head and shoulder fake maybe, or I'll move my foot a little way. O.K., my opponent sees through the fake. He's a smart guy; he knows doubles. And so I fake again and again, real early fakes that don't fool anyone. But on the next serve I fake early and this time I really "poach" and knock off the ball. I've made sure that I'm close to the net, so that I can make contact when the ball is at its highest point and I punch it either at the net man or through the opening in the center.

Faking and "poaching" are well worth cultivating for the disturbing effect they have on opponents. Apart from the points won by successful interceptions, the opponents may try so hard to make good returns they'll beat themselves. They'll try to outguess you and hit down your alley when you are not moving across, and, if the server is doing his job well enough, they won't pass you enough times to offset the value of your constant bluffing them at the net.

One of the best fakers—and I mean it in strictly a complimentary sense!—was Seixas, who got a lot of distance out of his game by his intelligence as well as his fitness and courage. We resorted to faking a great deal in our Davis Cup encounters with the Australians, encouraged by our captain, Talbert, who could see the possible deterioration in their returns of service. Against Hoad-Rosewall and Hoad-Hartwig we used a system of signals that conveyed the net man's intentions to the server. Maybe Vic signaled to me that he was going to cross. I served and took a couple of steps as though making directly for the net. Then I veered off into Vic's territory in case he had moved too early or the opponent had anticipated his move. I could still get to almost any ball, while Vic, if not outguessed, "poached" with demoralizing effect.

The position the four players take on the court should be well understood. The server takes up his position halfway between the sideline and the center mark, in contrast to singles in which he stands closer to the center. His partner stands about two small steps inside the singles sideline and about halfway between the service line and the net. Many players stand too close to the net and have no chance to react quickly enough to handle a fast ball. Moreover, they are vulnerable to a lob, and when a ball has passed over your head in doubles you have lost the offensive. You have given the net away!

The receiver in the first court should never stand farther back than the base line. If he's behind the base line he is not going to be able to return low often enough to hurt the fellow coming in to the net. He has a chance of reaching the net himself behind his return and a deep volley will have him scrambling about six feet behind the base line. He has to make a defensive lob which 99 per cent of the time will be killed.

The receiver's partner should stand just inside the service line. Some good players stand in a comparable position with the opposing net man, that is, halfway between the service line and the net. But the server's partner has the initiative; he knows where his partner will serve and he's looking for a high return. The receiver's partner, on the other hand, is defenseless if the ball is punched hard at him from an interception. The server racing into the net also has him at his mercy if the return is high.

I suggest the receiver's partner stand back a bit, therefore giving himself a fraction of a second longer in which to react. If the return is good all he has to do is take one or two steps forward and he's in an ideal offensive position to pick the ball off as it's rising over the net; a bad return, and he has a better chance of determining the direction of the opponent's shot without retreating. Any time a player retreats in doubles he's in trouble. He must try at all times to move his weight forward against the ball. It follows that the netman is more likely to stay in the action and play a telling volley if he leans forward while his partner's returning the service.

Now let's turn to the return of service in doubles. Most players agree that returning the ball from the first court is more difficult than from the second court, and normally it's the first-court player who controls the play. Possibly he won't hit the ball as hard, particularly off his backhand, but he should make sure he gets his return into play.

The reason Talbert and Hartwig were tremendous first-court players was their consistency. Off their forehands, they could hit top-spin, pulling the ball across at an angle, or aiming through the center, and nearly always to the server's feet. And they could take their backhands early on their way in to the net. They always gave their team a chance by keeping the ball in play.

Bromwich was another great player in the deuce court with his two-handed forehand and his left-handed stroke on the normal backhand side. Few of his returns were hit really hard, yet they were so low and accurate, no one was happy serving to him.

On a fairly fast surface the fellow receiving service in the first court should stand on or just inside the base line with his right foot close to or on the singles sideline. If he stands too far away from the sideline he's vulnerable to a ball sliced wide. Even if he reaches it, he's moving sideways and won't be able to hustle in behind his return. Moreover, he's left a big hole in the center. The receiver shouldn't have both heels parallel to the base line. He should turn so that he faces the server, enabling him to have an equal chance with shots on either side.

Normally, the top players don't take a full swing on their return of service because the ball is traveling too fast. Accuracy is more important than pace. The ball has to be kept away from the net man. It has to be kept low and moved around.

Use the speed on the ball. Take a short backswing—don't merely block the ball—and try to hit it low, or else chip it so that it floats over the net and falls short. Always keep in mind that you must try to make your opponents volley up.

The fellow returning from the ad court also stands on or inside the base line and both fellows, when returning service, lean forward ready to move into the ball. When I play in the ad court I stand with my left foot almost on the singles sideline. I don't like leaving too big an opening up the center in case the ball is sliced there. Neither do I like to have too far to run if the ball is served deep to the backhand corner.

At the start of the point the serving team is the aggressor. The receivers must try to snatch the offensive away from them by returning low and swarming to the net.

Following the return into the net puts pressure on the server, who many times may try to hit a low, soft volley to the feet. He may not hit it perfectly, either lofting it or hitting it short. His offensive position then has been jeopardized.

A high ball, as I said earlier, ought to be volleyed at the net man, but if there's any doubt that the shot may not be sufficiently

Jack Bromwich, perhaps tennis's outstanding right-hand court doubles player, here partnered with Frank Sedgman, demonstrates the two-handed forehand he played so effectively.

offensive to be an outright winner, by all means send the ball back to the man on the base line. This is assuming that the opposition is spread-eagled, one up, one back. The long trajectory of the ball from the base line gives you time to pick it off. If it's high you can step in and kill it.

In matches between good doubles teams all four players are frequently at the net together. The same principle of volleying at the nearest opponent applies, though if it's used without variation the opponents will decide that they can forget about the center and concentrate on covering themselves. To keep them honest it's necessary to vary your tactics.

"Keeping a fellow honest" is a phrase we use a lot. From the ad court, for instance, I'll hit a few returns at the net man, not because I want to be charitable—there is *no* charity in pro tennis —but because I want him to be aware that at any time I may hit there. He is not going to be so sure then about edging across and "poaching." That's what I mean by keeping him honest.

Let's look at a few hypothetical doubles situations. Say you're in the right court, you've returned the ball but aren't able to follow it in. Your opponent volleys back to you. Depending on the volley, you're just inside the base line or one or two yards behind it. Your shot now is extremely important, yet few players understand what they should try to do with this second shot.

If the ball is on your forehand you must *not* try to hit it straight up the alley. Even some of the best players attempt to do this and it is a bad mistake. It opens up the entire court. Consider the possibilities presented to the net man. He can volley back down the alley, because the receiver must move across to cover the gap in the center he's made by playing his shot. He can angle a volley through the center between both players. He can angle it directly onto the opposing net man, who will have difficulty handling such a sharply angled ball. Or he can hit a delicate short angle, which beats the net man because he has his weight on the right foot trying to cover that gap in the center. And so, by hitting that shot up the line you have trapped yourself. Of course, it may be done once in a while to keep the other guys honest—when they're 30-love or 40-15—but never when they're down love-30 or 15-40 and you have a chance of a service break.

What are the alternatives to the ball down the line? Well, one that can be tried is to hit to the net man's right hip. It will be difficult for him to angle this past his opposing net man. He either has to volley straight back or try to maneuver the ball into the center. A good partner, seeing the ball going to the net man, will move slightly into the center in an effort to make him volley straight back, thus allowing his partner to have another crack at the ball and this time either hitting directly at the man at the net from closer range or going for a winner through the center.

Try not to panic on your second shot when you are at the back of the court. There's a temptation to hit the ball with all your might, but a cool head and accuracy are more rewarding than blind power. A medium-paced ball, hit low, will seldom get you in trouble.

The safest second shot is down the center. If you can top the ball to make it dip, so much the better. It doesn't have to be hit too hard. Hitting to the center is safe; not only do you restrict your opponents' angle, but you may also cause some confusion. Both players may swing at the ball, or both may let it go.

Don't, whatever you do on the second shot, try to roll the ball across court, except on occasion to fool your opponents. This is as suicidal as the ball up the line, since it leaves your own court wide open.

The player covering that angle can hit a little angled drop shot or punch the ball hard at the man opposite him. If the player who has angled his drive moves up in anticipation of the drop shot, he leaves a hole in the center. If his partner tries to plug the hole in the center he leaves his alley unguarded.

The offensive lob is a distinct possibility as a second shot. Talbert played the offensive lob as well as anyone, especially on a ball wide on his forehand. He could make a lob down the sideline, just clearing the man at the net. Even if he jumped and reached the ball, it was high on his backhand and he couldn't do much with it. The other offensive lob, diagonally over the server's head, can be hit harder because the diagonal gives you more court in which to hit.

Let's swap sides for a moment and imagine that we are on the receiving end of such a lob. The server must use all his speed to reach the net, but in doing so he is vulnerable to the offensive lob.

It's his partner's responsibility to defend against that lob, moving back if possible and smashing it to maintain the offensive position. Unless he's prepared for this contingency, the team can be in real trouble. The player cross-court to the ball has the choice of moving in closer to the net or not. His partner holds his position.

Don't stand and admire your lobs. If you've managed to get an offensive lob over the opposition, move in quickly to prevent them from recapturing the ground they've lost. They may play a defensive lob, which you should be able to put away, or they may hit a ground stroke, which you can volley from the net position.

I recommend letting the very high lobs drop, because the ball is falling straight down. Once it has landed and bounced into the air again it will descend more slowly. You have a better chance of timing it well. There is no great advantage in hitting the ball in the air before it bounces because your opponents have had time to recover into a good position anyway. They've hit it high to give themselves time to get into a good position and attempt to retrieve your smash.

Naturally, some points in doubles are more important than others, just as in singles. When the opposition is down 15-40, for instance, the guy in the deuce court *must* get that ball back into play, even if he hits it a little high. The pressure is on the pair struggling to hold service. Don't remove that pressure by attempting a super shot that hits the net or goes out. Make them beat you—don't beat yourself!

Some people tend to think that the better player takes over the ad court in order to play the last point in each game. But this doesn't make sense. If the weaker player is in the deuce court a team may never get to advantage. It takes two to make a team!

Determining which side of the court to take hinges on individual stroke equipment. Some players can hit their backhands outward from the deuce court toward the server's alley. Others can't. I find it difficult the way I hit my backhand. It is easier for me to roll a backhand cross-court, and I prefer to slide my forehand out, though I can top it when necessary.

Talbert was perfect in the deuce court because he could slice his backhand or block it or give it top-spin to make it dip low, and he could also roll over a forehand.

The fellow on the backhand side should have an offensive

backhand return of service, which he can roll or under-spin. Rose-wall is an example of a player who hits an under-spin backhand with great success, taking it on the rise and moving in.

Every doubles pair must try to move as a unit, and when thrown on defense cover their opponents' best shots and force them to attempt the awkward ones. A guy like Hoad prefers to smash into the backhand corner. My partner and I know this. He knows we know it! But he can't do anything to stop me lobbing and covering that smash to the backhand. He's tempted to smash the other way. If he's good enough to make it, well, he deserves the point. But a lot of the time he'll elect to play his natural shot, which we have covered. Eventually we may pick up several points which we otherwise would have lost.

When you have the opportunity, therefore, make your opponents do what they don't like to do. By covering their best shots, you may make them resort to their second choice on which they have less confidence and success.

People may wonder why a player like Gonzales doesn't bang that big service down all the time. He only has to do it four times and he's won a game. Well, you can name all your great players and not one was capable of getting all his first serves into court. In good doubles, provided the conditions are satisfactory, players often will return the fastest balls. Then there is so much pace on the ball that the server coming in for the return is caught behind the service line with the ball at his feet. He doesn't have time to get into the ideal volleying position.

There's another thing to remember—when your big serve fails, no chances can be taken with the second serve. That may result in your serving a little short with a high enough bounce to allow the receiver to take the offensive.

Good hard spin and varied spin is preferable to an overplayed booming service. I believe in pounding down flat serves once in a while hoping for an ace or a weak return. Then when I think I have a receiver static, waiting, I throw some slow spin at him. I have time to get to the net while he has to generate his own speed from the base line.

If I'm serving to a player like Hoad I can't spin every ball to his backhand or he will step in and hurt me. I must move my serve around. Say he's playing in the ad court. I will try to serve very wide and deep to his backhand side. Sometimes I may serve straight at him. At other times I may hit two or three cannonball serves, which I hope will leave him uncertain, and waiting for more. Then I'll go back to my spin serve, hoping to surprise him, and keep him from moving in.

The half volley is a difficult but valuable shot in doubles. When executed well it can turn defense into offense, but a bad half volley puts you at your opponents' mercy. The thing to remember is not to hit the half volley hard or the ball will fly high above the net. As you come into the net and the return falls to your feet, try to hit the ball softly so that it goes back to the feet of the incoming opponent. If you can make him in turn volley up, you have hit a fine shot. Often it's advisable to hit the half volley toward the fellow at the net, because, unless he's an excellent doubles player, he probably will be standing still. He shouldn't be; he should be moving forward to ram home the advantage. But if he is static, a half volley at him may be effective.

Many players make the mistake when serving into the deuce court of volleying the return up the alley. Even though once in a while it may work, as in the case of the attempted drive up the alley, this is unwise because the whole of your court is opened up. A good doubles player will be onto that ball and he will knock it right through you. But you can't do the same thing all the time, even if it's tactically correct. Smart players will anticipate and take advantage of your lack of imagination. You must be intelligent and change your tactics while remaining fundamentally sound.

For example, I serve five times to the same guy in the deuce court and I come into the net. Five times he puts the ball a little high on my forehand. O.K. I can play five different shots. I can volley back very deep to the base line. He's made a bad return, so he's not going to try to come in behind it. If he does I hit hard down at his feet and I've certainly won the point. I can hit a high forehand volley through the center. The man at the net has got to freeze. He must defend his own position. I can hit the ball onto the net man's right hip. I can hit it on his left side. And I can hit it at his feet. On the same ball very occasionally I can also hit a drop volley even though the ball is high;

I don't normally favor drop shots in doubles, because one opponent is on the base line and the other is static at the net. But if on that ball I had hit through the center five times, the net man will take note. Maybe when I'm down 15-40 he'll move into the center and pick off my shot, knocking it straight at me. I'm trapped. I've done something technically sound, but I've done it too many times. So vary your tactics. Once in a while you should hit your second shot down the alley or angled, just to keep the opposition honest. Have the game score to your advantage when you do it, however!

I don't like lob volleys in doubles. They may come off sometimes, but if you make a habit of playing them you'll play them by reflex when you should be playing an offensive volley. The best doubles players only resort to lob volleys when they are in extreme difficulty at the net. Perhaps an opponent has hit a low angle to the feet and knowing that he's moving into the net a player will try to lift the volley over him. Obviously, there is a lot of risk in such an ambitious shot. You might end up eating the ball!

As you may have gathered by now I abhor risks in tennis. All the pros do. When we play doubles we try to eliminate unnecessary risks. If you do, too, you'll find yourself winning many more matches.

Frank Sedgman

Conditioning, Temperament, and Equipment

Don't let anyone ever fool you that the best players of the past were superior to the champions of the postwar years. They could not have been. They were not as fit.

As far as I can gather lawn tennis in the old days was a game of skill and grace rather than speed and stamina. Of course, there must have been fit, strong players. Fred Perry, no doubt, was as athletic as they come. But the pace of living was slower, the jet plane hadn't shrunk the world, players had more time to travel or relax between tournaments and the game hadn't been systematically analyzed.

Then Jack Kramer and Harry Hopman came along. Kramer convinced every thinking person that athleticism allied to the serve-volley game wins every time. A few years later Hopman took over control of Australia's Davis Cup campaigns, putting into effect his belief in high-powered conditioning. Since then

Australian lawn tennis has been synonymous with fitness. The Australian champions have been strong, lithe young men, not always endowed with the most brilliant strokes, but confident in their ability to survive the most grueling matches on the hottest, most wearing of days.

During the last few Wimbledon tournaments it has been pointed out that Australians have the knack of pulling out victory in the fifth set after being on the verge of defeat. Rod Laver, Neale Fraser, Roy Emerson and Bob Hewitt are among those I recall pulling their matches out of the fire. Good temperament helped, but all the temperament in the world isn't of much avail if you run out of steam. Laver, Fraser and company won largely because they were more robust and lasted the distance better than their opponents.

Players these days need speed, strength, quick reflexes, flexibility and stamina if they are going to play with top efficiency throughout an entire match lasting maybe two to three hours. It is no use thinking these qualities will be acquired in the normal course of playing tennis. They have to be sought objectively. If they are not sought and obtained, players will find themselves being defeated by opponents who are not as skillful, but who are in better physical condition—and that is sheer waste of talent.

When Hopman inaugurated his "chain gang," as the Americans put it, he had a few players who heartily disliked the drudgery of training. Among them were Mervyn Rose and George Worthington, both of whom might have got closer to the Wimbledon crown and Davis Cup triumphs had they buckled down to some solid work and made themselves fitter.

Dick Savitt, the big American, was another player who loathed training and who clashed with his Davis Cup team captain, Frank Shields, in Australia over his refusal to do exercises with the rest of the team. Sure I know Savitt won the Wimbledon title. I think with all his great ability, however, he could have won much more.

Today it is a shame to see so many other talented players limiting themselves by their sluggishness. The Italian, Nicola Pietrangeli, has some of the most attractive strokes in the game, but they are not always utilized because he is patently unfit. When he came to Australia in Italian Davis Cup teams he sometimes donned a track suit with the intention of training, yet usually what he did was ludicrous. He merely jogged about a bit, touched his toes a few times—and then knocked off for a plate of spaghetti. His condition in the heat didn't allow him to do his strokes justice.

Britain's Bobby Wilson is another whose condition is very suspect. Had he prepared himself for tournaments thoroughly, he might have improved on his record of causing an occasional upset at Wimbledon, and actually won a few major titles.

For the point that must be stressed is that a hard, dependable body induces a cool, confident state of mind. A player who doesn't have to worry about seeing out a match can really get on with the job.

The best place in which to build up your body methodically is in a gymnasium, and I'm not saying that simply because I own one! I am certain that without all those hours exerting myself in a gym I would never have achieved the success I did.

I started going to the gym I now own when I was fourteen, doing body building with heavy weights. Much of it was set work—that is, lifting a heavy weight in three batches, with each batch consisting of ten lifts. I worked out for about an hour or an hour and a half three or four times a week after school or after work at the Melbourne Argus newspaper office. So much work admittedly slowed me down, but that didn't matter; I was building up strength and power. When a tournament was coming around I knocked off the strength work, because it would have affected my speed and rhythm, and switched to speed and flexibility exercises.

Nowadays, when a tennis player comes to my gym for advice and instruction, his requirements are assessed by one of the most astute physical culturists in the business, Stan Nichols. The player is asked how much time he wants to devote to training and whether he has any special targets, such as an important tournament. Then Stan compiles a course to suit him.

If he is heavy in the legs and hips and has a comparatively weak upper body, he will be given agility and flexibility movements for his legs. These will improve his spring, suppleness and endurance. What we call "stripping-down exercises" and flexibility movements will be prescribed to streamline his hips. For

A vicious overhead is certainly one of the shots in tennis which calls for the greatest agility and body coordination. Frank Sedgman's passion for physical fitness pays off when he can execute a smash like this one.

his upper body there will be other exercises, some of which will be designed specifically to pack power into his service, his forehand and his backhand. His abdominal muscles will be strengthened and, if he's keen enough, special running schedules will be devised for him.

It is thought mistakenly by some people that suppleness is something you either are born with or never possess in your life. Certainly, some athletes are naturally supple. I'm thinking in particular of Queenslanders raised in a hot climate that seems to loosen their joints. Watch the India-rubber gait of Malcolm Anderson, Roy Emerson, Rod Laver and Ken Fletcher, and you'll see what I mean. But other players can lose some of their stiffness by stretching exercises, and they can do other exercises that will pep up their muscle tone in all muscle groups.

When I say that we suggest running schedules for those who are keen enough, I hope that I am not giving the impression that running is not strictly essential. Every young player should try to incorporate some running into his training, because it is so good for stamina and wind. I realize, however, that in many countries with severe winters it demands a great deal of will power to go running for a few miles before or after work.

Where practical, players should start their running program two or three months before the tournament season opens. As a lot of running may tighten leg muscles and cause fatigue in a match, it is better to taper off shortly before the season opens and then to run only occasionally when no big matches are on hand. It was Hopman who established beyond any doubt the benefits of running, and the time Australian Davis Cup teams put in running over paddocks in their track suits can't be more profitably spent.

As in golf and cricket, strong wrists and hands are required in tennis. The part that a firm wrist plays in all strokes has been emphasized in other chapters of this book. There are several ways a player can strengthen his forearm, wrist and fingers. Margaret Smith, for instance, has done a lot of finger-strengthening exercises, including press-ups with all the weight on her fingers alone. Dumbbells must also be used if the wrist is weak, for a player will be unable to express the power he has built up through other muscle groups in his body if his delivering capability is deficient.

All these exercises generally apply to women as well as men, though with women supervision is necessary because the wrong type of exercises will merely give them bulk without efficiency. Margaret Smith has worked hard in the gym and done a fair amount of running. Her superior fitness has helped her to become the world's number one woman player. If you compare her with most of the other leading women players you can see that she runs to the ball faster, hits harder and maintains pressure much longer. Players such as Maria Bueno, Darlene Hard and Renee Schuurman are reasonably fit through playing tennis constantly, but as far as I know they don't go in for any training off the court, and this is why I think Margaret will always have an edge on them.

Adequate sleep and a sensible diet are two other ingredients of fitness. When I was on my way up the championship ladder I made sure I never had less than eight hours' sleep a night. Often my quota was ten hours, and others—Ken Rosewall for instance—slept closer to twelve. There have been playboys who have combined late nights with a reasonably successful tennis career. Art Larsen was one. And so to a certain extent was Ted Schroeder. They were the exceptions to the rule, for the majority of champions have a healthy respect for the demands of the game and don't handicap themselves by lack of sufficient rest.

As for diet, it's best to eat normal, well-balanced meals, keeping off fatty and fried foods and not eating too many starchy foods. High-protein foods are always preferable, though a player burns up so much energy that some starch in his diet won't do any harm. The average Australian goes in for salads, milk and fruit, which are hard to beat.

Faced with a hard match, it is well to plan your meals for the day. If you were scheduled to play at 2 P.M., I'd suggest for breakfast something like poached eggs or tomatoes on toast, plus a couple of slices of wholemeal bread and honey; and for lunch, two or three hours before the match, a light meal, possibly again eggs lightly poached on toast. At this stage—just prior to the match—carbohydrates are more useful than proteins as they provide almost instant energy.

I would advocate no smoking. It is definitely harmful. Medically, I think its effect on the lungs has been established beyond doubt. If you can't breathe freely you won't get far in any sport that entails exertion. Maybe a person who likes smoking four or five cigarettes a day won't perceptibly jeopardize his form, but if a player wants to eliminate all unnecessary risks I say emphatically, don't smoke.

There is less risk in alcohol, so long as it is taken in moderation. In fact, alcohol can be beneficial, relieving tension and aiding the nervous system to settle down after an exhausting match. Never take alcohol before a match and never to excess at any time. Apart from anything else, it deadens the nervous system, which is disastrous in a high-speed game such as tennis. Most of the top professionals enjoy a few beers after their matches, but few of them drank before they were mature players. I didn't touch alcohol until I was about twenty-eight and I have never smoked. In this respect I think that in the top league I'm pretty average.

Squash can be quite helpful in conditioning a tennis player and I advocate it in those climates where winter tennis is not practicable. It is good for wind, stamina and quickness, but bad for footwork and stroking generally. Young players, particularly, shouldn't play squash at the same time as tennis because they will pick up bad habits. In the last few years I have played a lot of squash and enjoyed it. However, I've found myself taking squash shots onto the tennis court. I have consciously had to discard them, for a wristy squash action gives no control over the ball in tennis.

Cramp is sometimes associated with unfitness, though I'm not sure that this can be proved. It may be that in the lower brackets of the game the unfit player is more prone to cramp than the player in good condition. On the other hand, the fittest champions who try to push themselves beyond their physical capabilities can be struck down.

Both in 1961 and 1962 Margaret Smith suffered cramps during the French championships. No other woman was as fit as she. Ted Schroeder used to get cramps in his racket hand. One year in the first round of Wimbledon he got a cramp playing Gardnar Mulloy and at the time I put it down to nervousness. Earl Buchholz might have had his name on the Wimbledon roll now but for the cramp to which he's vulnerable, and he's as fit as they come. But Dick Savitt and Mervyn Rose suffered cramps—and they were not fit.

Salt tablets are usually recommended for those who cramp in the heat of a tough match. Playing in the tropics, it is usually wise to have them on the court with you—especially if you perspire unduly. I'm not sure that the main value I've drawn from salt tablets is not psychological. (If you think something is doing you good, take it!) The Australian Davis Cup team, however, is never without a supply of salt tablets on humid days, and at Brisbane against the Mexicans in 1962 Rod Laver, Roy Emerson and Neale Fraser all resorted to them.

In top-class tennis a lot of success hinges on sharp reflexes—the time it takes the eye to see the ball, transmit the right message to the brain, and then for the brain to operate the muscle.

I'm not going to try to fool you. You are either born with sharp reflexes or you are not. Either you see the ball coming early and respond instinctively or you don't see it until it's on you and then act laboriously. However, reflexes can be sharpened to some extent with volleying exercises and with skipping, jumping and other exercises to speed the mental processes and footwork.

Ashley Cooper realized that his reflexes didn't match those of Lew Hoad and Ken Rosewall. He went in for all these exercises, but though he has improved his reflexes, they are still inferior to Hoad's and Rosewall's.

Hoad is uncanny in the way he can flick his wrist to pick up balls that appear to be past him. But today Rosewall has the outstanding reflexes. It is said that he takes eye exercises to enable him to see moving objects more quickly. Knowing what a methodical little fellow he is I can quite believe it.

For a big man, my old doubles partner Ken McGregor had splendid reflexes, as did Pancho Gonzales in his prime, and Art Larsen. The most amazing reflex man of them all was John Bromwich, who could move his racket into awkward positions so quickly that you thought he was employing black magic.

When anticipation is combined with sharp reflex actions the result is devastating. In my last few years as an amateur it was my anticipation and ability to move in the right direction to cut off passing shots that gave me perhaps my greatest advantage over other competitors.

Anticipation comes largely from watching the opponent's body position. Coming to the net behind a shot, I can see the direction in which the ball is going to come back by the way the opponent moves into the ball, by the way he moves his shoulders and hips. The angle I have hit and his initial movement toward it is often enough. It is all largely instinctive.

Bromwich was a brute to play because he hit everything off

Frank Sedgman hasn't waited for the ball to come to him, but has anticipated so well that he's starting to move up into the forecourt at the same
moment that he is about to blast a forehand from deep court.

the wrong foot, particularly on his left-handed side, and kept his opponent guessing. He did scarcely anything the way the average player does it and, consequently, coming to the net against him, you just couldn't anticipate.

Hoad is the same. He hits with his wrist and with less body movement than most players. He can hit the ball from any position off either foot, and he makes anticipation extremely hard for his opponent.

Against orthodox players anticipation is made up of studying shoulders and hips, assessing the way the racket is held, the racket angle, and the way the wrist is coming into the shot. Against unorthodox players your guess is as good as mine.

Despite all the injunctions to watch the ball don't be afraid to take your eye off it when your opponent is making his stroke. You must watch it after he has made contact, but until then look at the way he is moving and how he is shaping up.

Speed at the net comes from natural pace plus bounding ability. Many players are flat-footed at the net, lacking both pace and spring. Bromwich, for instance, was never very impressive at the net, except in doubles when he didn't have so much court to cover. In singles he was often stranded at the net by his inability to spring and cut the ball off. When he tried to spring he barely got a few inches off the ground, whereas players such as Ken McGregor and Don Candy could jump feet into the air for a smash at a fraction of a second's notice.

Roy Emerson is another who is gifted with an immense spring and a fine sense of timing, as well as lightning movements on the ground. As a good schoolboy sprinter and high-jumper, he had certain natural advantages to start with.

A part of my volleying technique in the fifties was to leave a little more space on the forehand side to tempt my opponent to hit there, because my forehand volley was stronger. Once I got my racket on the ball I generally made sure of hitting a winner. I don't know that it was such a wonderful idea. Sometimes I left so much space on the forehand side, and my opponent played such a fine shot, that my purpose was defeated.

Ken Rosewall, of course, leaves more space on his backhand side. His backhand volley, like his backhand ground stroke, is very strong—though his forehand volley is far from weak.

If there is an outstanding strength in which a player has supreme confidence it seems good sense to exploit it. Some players don't seem to know which is their better volley and they haven't a clue about holding out bait. They just don't think about their game. If you think you have an unbeatable stroke I suggest you take a few risks with it—but not at the sacrifice of building up your other strokes.

Much hinges, of course, on the type of game the opponent plays, and in this respect it is always well worthwhile to study matches in which future opponents may be engaged. Over the last decade or so Davis Cup captains such as Harry Hopman and Bill Talbert have refined the art of dissecting rival players to gain knowledge of their strengths and weaknesses for use in Challenge Rounds. Individuals can help themselves in tournaments if they make an effort to watch and learn about other competitors in the early rounds.

I played Vic Seixas a number of times in my amateur days and soon realized that he invariably tried to hit his backhand down the line. As a professional, I discovered Jack Kramer was the same, though he was certainly capable of making a fine cross-court backhand. On the other hand, Ken Rosewall early in his career used to hit both backhand and forehand across court. Knowing that these were their strongest shots, and that under pressure they would play them almost automatically, enabled me to anticipate them. I would go to the net behind a shot to Seixas' backhand and concentrate on his drive down the line. The same with Kramer. Naturally they tried to foil me, but generally they leaned so heavily on their favorite shot that when they essayed the alternative they failed. And so the next development was for me to leave a little opening to tempt them to make their favorite shot—being 99 per cent sure they couldn't resist the invitation—and then anticipate it.

Sometimes I think that good anticipation is synonymous with confidence. A player anticipating his opponent's shots and dominating the net is brimful of confidence, while his opponent's confidence wanes proportionately. If, however, a player is all at sea in picking the direction of shots, he frets, loses confidence and invariably loses.

One of the most important factors in the best class of tennis

Frank Sedgman has purposely left a little opening on his backhand to tempt a shot to him on that side. The plan has worked, and he is about to punch away his volley to the right-hand corner of Trabert's court.

is concentration. Few of the champions lack it. Kramer, Gonzales, Segura and Rosewall were able to concentrate relentlessly from the start of their careers.

Hoad is an exception. When he is concentrating 100 per cent he is well-nigh unbeatable, but when he is only half concentrating he can fall to a far inferior player. It has always been the same with Lew. As an amateur he was superb on the big occasions, such as a Davis Cup Challenge Round or Wimbledon final, because he was keyed-up to pull out his best and wanted to win as quickly as possible. In many less important matches, against players far short of his class, his mind was not always on the job. He made careless errors and either lost, or scrambled home in the last set. As a professional he has remained erratic, though again, when he feels the challenge is worthy of him (his first matches with Rod Laver, for instance) he concentrates perfectly.

Laver has a similar temperament. Only in his last year as an amateur did he start to concentrate properly, hence his big improvement. Before 1962 his mind wandered, though perhaps not as much as Hoad's. Lew used to allow umpiring decisions and noisy spectators to disturb him, whereas Laver's amateur career was never marred by this sort of incident.

Nobody could adopt any better models in concentration than Kramer, Rosewall and Segura, who had and still have the knack of obliterating all extraneous matters from their minds when on court.

Concentration, I admit, never came easily to me. It required a conscious effort—especially in the big matches. I went out on the court telling myself not to allow the ballboys, the umpires, the spectators, the wind or anything else to upset me; I had to keep calm and concentrate on watching the ball, on footwork and on beating the other fellow. I knew that once I tensed up over outside influences I was on the road to defeat.

In a close match any little thing can throw a man out of stride if he's not firm with himself. A ballboy dropping a ball as you're about to serve, perspiration dripping into your eyes, or the umpire making an obvious mistake—all these things in the heat of a match may be magnified out of all proportion. They nag at you at the back of your mind and, although you know they are interfering with your performance, it is hard to forget them.

With determination, however, every player can improve his concentration. The operative word is "determination." Make up your mind that you will never take your mind off the match until it is over. If there are other matches alongside yours ignore them— even though there may be a lull for some reason in your own match. The only time you should give any sign that any other player in the club exists is when another ball rolls onto the court.

Bromwich is the player who's had the best concentration in my time. He was even more single-minded than Kramer, Rosewall and Segura. Nothing shook him. Of the champions, Hoad and Laver have suffered most from loose concentration. Ted Schroeder was notorious for concentrating hard only in the fourth and fifth sets of matches. He could have won in straight sets had he willed it.

Like all games, tennis demands a positive approach. A player who goes into a match expecting to be beaten *will* be beaten. He must think he is going to win even though his opponent's record is greatly superior. Bill Talbert used to drill the value of the positive approach into his players when he was Davis Cup captain. Tony Trabert and Barry MacKay exemplified it in their attitudes. MacKay hadn't done much before Talbert surprisingly selected him to play in a Challenge Round at Melbourne and convinced him that he could beat anyone in the world. As a result, MacKay played his opening match against the more experienced Malcolm Anderson as though he were the favorite, not the Australian, and came very close to causing a big upset.

The champions never allow themselves to doubt that they will win. They may be two sets down and still be certain of victory. The mediocre players, meanwhile, may be in command of a match until they miss an easy volley or serve a double fault. Doubt creeps into their minds, they tighten up and they collapse.

I always worked on the theory that I would win every match I played. Maybe I said to people before going onto the court that I didn't fancy my chances, but in my innermost heart I always felt I would win. Not that overconfidence or cockiness is to be esteemed; the overconfident player looks upon all his opponent's good shots as lucky, doesn't give credit for them and loses his objectivity. There should be a balance between cockiness and the positive approach.

If a player doesn't have a strong will to win he will never survive the fierceness of championship tennis. I say that he hasn't got that will to win if he's not prepared to make sacrifices such as giving up late nights, movies and the wrong kind of food. A coach can tell whether a protégé is going to fight out hard matches on the court by the youngster's willingness to prepare himself thoroughly beforehand, forgoing all pleasures except the pleasure of achieving his ambition.

A lot of the present crop of amateur players look for excuses to give a match away. If they are fully fit, there are no excuses.

They should be able to take the bad breaks with the good and overcome those bad breaks, because generally they even out. It's tough when a bad break comes on a vital point, but it has to be accepted. The only policy is to keep trying to swing the match around and then perhaps the luck will change.

Some very good players throw sets and still maintain the resolve to win. They hope to recover their strength for a final desperate throw in the fourth or fifth sets and haven't really weakened in their determination. I don't go along with these tactics because I think they are unnecessary and dangerous if a man has maximum fitness. The opponent wins points without much exertion and his confidence may soar to such an extent that he is a vastly improved player by the time the deciding set comes along.

Combined with single-mindedness and unshakable will to win is sportsmanship, not simply because it is right, but because it is sensible. If you play the game as it should be played without ever becoming ruffled and your opponent knows you will never be ruffled you are not giving him an advantage.

Tenseness and irritability only reduce efficiency. Quite often I've seen my opponent angrily let fly with a ball or his racket and my reaction has been to put on the pressure. Obviously he was upset, his concentration gone. Now was the time to get on top and perhaps win the match by one service break. By losing his temper he had played into my hands.

In the professional ranks, of course, most of the boys have mastered the knack of never becoming ruffled. It is rare that you see a bad-tempered pro. Fellows like Hoad, MacKay and Buchholz come into the professional game with reputations for whacking their rackets into the court and knocking balls out of the stadium. They soon learn the hard way that these tantrums are costly.

When the competition is tough no one can afford to give the other fellow a start by doing his block, because the odds are he will never catch up. All the older pros have been through the mill and when they see a racket flying around they take it as a sure sign they've got their man where they want him.

I know there is a theory that to explode and let off steam relieves the tension. The game is played on a relatively small surface area which sometimes is surrounded by a wall of faces, so that it is understandable that some players feel a claustrophobic pressure building up within them.

Bob Hewitt, Dennis Ralston and Chuck McKinley are three young men who have all struck trouble for succumbing to the temptation to blow up under what they imagine is provocation. But what good has it done them? When they discipline themselves and show restraint they achieve better results.

We've all felt frustrated and angry on the tennis court at some time or other, but we are not going to gain much relief by taking it out on the racket, the ball, the net or the court! At one time I tried bouncing my racket to see if it helped me lose my annoyance at a muffed shot. It didn't. My concentration merely slipped further. Since then I've been convinced that when a player starts banging the equipment around in a fit of temper he has temporarily had a mental blockage and lost sight of his main aim, which is to win points by hitting the ball over the net.

Finally, I'd like to emphasize that the players who reach the highest pinnacles of the game are completely dedicated. Jack Kramer, Maureen Connolly, Ken Rosewall, Ashley Cooper, Margaret Smith, Rod Laver—all made up their minds when they were young to make sacrifices, work hard and become as fit as possible. They had loads of talent as well, of course. But talent alone is not enough.

Don Budge

Playing Winning Tennis After Fifty

Not so long ago I was playing in a mixed doubles tournament at a Los Angeles tennis club. It was a handicap event, and my partner was a novice who somehow contrived to hit the ball with everything except the middle of the racket. Oh, how that girl suffered! She became increasingly nervous as every ball she hit went flying out of court. She must have thought an apology was called for. "Golly, Mr. Budge," she said, "this is going to set your game back about ten years." I said, "Well, I certainly hope so."

You can look at this little reminiscence in a couple of ways. Firstly, lawn tennis is to be played for fun, and don't forget it. It is not a grim, life-and-death business, no matter how hard some of our leading players try to pretend it is in tournament play. Secondly, the older player shouldn't try to fool himself. When he gets into his fifties and sixties there is no substitute for youth. Sure, he has experience, judgment, discretion. But none of it will save him if he's on court against a class player who has speed and power.

Lawn tennis is a game for men and women of all ages so long

as they keep their sense of proportion. Former King Gustav V of Sweden played until he was eighty-eight. That should be enough encouragement for anyone that the game can be played for a lifetime.

Most of the good clubs around the world have elderly members whose lives would be very dull indeed without their regular doubles and mixed doubles. Why, I'm told that at Kooyong in Australia one of the keenest players is an arthritically crippled old gentleman who makes his way onto court with a walking stick. Come hot or cold weather, or the arrival of big crowds to watch Davis Cup and championship matches on the center court, nothing can stop him from playing regularly with his cronies. Of course, he doesn't attempt to chase anything. He knows his limitations. And this is the big point to remember. You are not going to derive any fun from the game if you overextend yourself. You can continue playing lawn tennis as long as you feel up to getting out on the court. But take it easy. Play within yourself. Don't run frantically after those wide balls.

Competitive tennis in the big league started to become too much for me in my late thirties. When I reached forty I decided then and there that the high-pressure game was for youngsters, that it was time for me to get out of the competitive end and go into business. Most of my better-known contemporaries—Jack Crawford, Fred Perry, Gottfried von Cramm—made similar decisions about the same age. But Jean Borotra shamed all of us by continuing to play mixed doubles at Wimbledon into his sixties; by his enthusiasm and dedication to physical fitness he remains an inspiration to all middle-aged players.

I still enjoy the game, but, of course, I miss shots now that I would never have missed when I was younger. I don't expect to compete with the Hoads, Rosewalls and Lavers, yet it is a little sad when I go onto the court and muff a ball that I would have dispatched with contempt in the old days. It is one of the penalties one pays for having been lucky enough to be a champion. From the peak there is only one path—downward. But, what the heck! As I say, I still get a great deal of fun out of my tennis, muffed shots and all.

Whether a fellow continues to play singles as he advances into middle age depends on his physical condition. Only he can really know. If he can play singles and not become too tired there's no reason why he shouldn't keep going.

It is useless being emphatic about what one should and should not do at a certain age. There are too many guys around ready to prove that feeling old is a state of mind. I have known some great middle-aged singles players. Bill Tilden was one, and today there are Pancho Segura and Gardnar Mulloy.

To be honest, however, I guess one of the reasons they are so great is that their bodies are more youthful than those of the average fellows of their age. Their youthful suppleness has helped them to remain great competitors and beat others in the same age group who were perhaps better players in their prime. So let's recognize it: some middle-aged players are lucky; they're endowed with youthful bodies. And some work much harder at retaining a youthful body than most of us are prepared to do.

It has been put to me sometimes that a top-class player can beat the up-and-coming younger man by sheer touch and strategy. The case is quoted of Norman Brookes, the famous Australian left-hander, who at the age of forty-four gave Bill Tilden a tough four-set Davis Cup match when Tilden was in his vigorous twenties. It must be remembered, though, that in those days amateur tennis was the biggest and most important part of tennis. Professional tennis had not yet made serious inroads into the world's pool of amateur talent, and good players lasted longer.

Nowadays a player of any class normally has turned professional by the time he is twenty-four or twenty-five, and unlike old soldiers who fade away, he is usually killed off around thirty. The tremendous demands of professional tennis have eliminated the possibility of a top-class veteran in his forties giving a good youngster a battle.

Personally, I don't think any older fellow can hope to hold his own with the younger fellows. I don't think he should even try to attempt it.

What, then, should be his attitude as he grows older and realistically faces the fact that he is not a potential Wimbledon champion any more? Well, if he's a hard hitter he should continue hitting the ball hard, hoping to win points quickly. He should not try to play beyond himself and certainly not try to serve cannonballs, because the older you get the harder it becomes to serve a clean ace. Even Pancho Gonzales, who has the biggest service in the world, doesn't try to serve as many aces as he did when a youngster. A lot of tournament players have burned themselves out at an early age because of their overreliance on a booming service. As they aged, their service took too much out of them. Their condition gave out and they had nothing left. My advice is to groove a safe, steady service, with good depth and direction, which might not win points outright, but which will command respect.

The older player doesn't necessarily have to give up the serve-volley game. If he's reasonably fit and agile, he should by all means go into the net and use his volley. If continually running to and from the net is too great an exertion, then he has to rely more on the base-line game, waiting and working for errors from his opponent instead of forcing winners in the forecourt.

In doubles, of course, it is imperative to make the net position. Even among us creaky old-timers, doubles is won and lost at the net, and so we must hustle in there as effectively as we can. Now if you serve a little more easily you can generally get in closer to the net, because the ball takes that much longer to reach the opposition and come back. A nice, easy spinning serve onto the receiver's backhand will do just fine.

Even so, he may handle the shot well. You may find yourself half-volleying a lot more balls than you did when you were younger and could speed into the net like a gazelle. The main thing to remember is not to try to do too much with the half volley. Try to get the ball up over the net and then down onto your opponent's feet, so that he in turn is faced with the danger of hitting up at you. He can miss a ball just as easily as you. So don't deny him the opportunity. Forget thoughts of winning with half volleys.

The veteran has to make the best of whatever physical and mental equipment he has at his disposal. Occasionally, he is going to come up against a younger player who puts much more zip into his shots. Should he try to pep up the pace of his own shots in an effort to outgun his opponent? No, he should simply try to keep the ball going back, striking it as he normally does. The younger guy, hitting hard, will probably overhit on many occasions. He'll make as many mistakes as winners. If he doesn't,

The style of clothing and a few other things have changed in the twenty years since Don Budge started to powder one forehand drive in the early 1940s (ABOVE) and when he finished blasting another in the 1960s (BELOW). But the grace, form and enjoyment he brings to the game are exactly the same.

he's going to win the match anyway. Philosophically admit that he can hit the ball harder. Try primarily to keep sending it back, for this alone will put him under pressure.

Any player of caliber understands the value of spin, guile and the element of surprise. Mastering these qualities is a matter of experience, but it is foolish to think they can see you through if you have not had a grounding in the fundamentals of the game, or if you ignore the principles of percentage tennis outlined elsewhere in this book.

The best way to learn lawn tennis is from the bottom up. Don't think you can get by with short cuts. Learn the fundamentals, because in the long run the results will justify the trouble that is taken. Even in middle age, a man or woman starting to play the game for the first time is better off by persevering with the orthodox strokes. He or she won't execute them as well, perhaps, as the younger player or players who received coaching in the orthodox strokes when they were young, but with practice they will see themselves making a steady improvement and they will gain the maximum fun. Once they appreciate the importance of standing sideways to the net, pivoting and making the racket do all the work with a smooth rhythmical swing, they will be eager to play more often.

I admit that it is not too much fun for older people to go out and practice a stroke here and there without playing a game. After all, they can't be expected to have the same dedication as youngsters. But playing the game in a haphazard, clueless way is so much more tiring, as well as being ineffective. If they learn a few of the basic things they will enjoy the game more—and their opponents will enjoy it less!

Naturally, I don't advocate that players should attempt to hit the ball off the correct foot *all* the time. There are some fine players with wonderful ball sense who can hit shots from positions in which others would be off balance. I maintain, however, that the average player of any age should hit the ball off the correct foot 95 per cent of the time, and this he will do if he has learned to approach the ball in the proper way. Five per cent of the time he will have to deal with the ball as best he can, making his stroke when in an unsound position.

The players in the highest class of lawn tennis who find themselves hitting shots off the wrong foot more often than 5 per cent of the time are exceptions to the rule. Give me a good, orthodox player hitting off the correct foot and he will gain better results ninety-nine times out of a hundred.

Similarly, what we know about percentage tennis doesn't lose any force when applied to the older players' games. Any time anyone tries to do anything well he has to play the percentages. If he doesn't, he's kidding himself—not using his common sense.

A couple of deficiencies in most older players are poorer eyesight and an expanding girth. Together, they form quite a hazard.

The parrot cry in lawn tennis is, as it is in all ball games, keep your eye on the ball. What with slower reflexes and diminished sight, this injunction cannot always be obeyed. Certainly, it is not possible for most of us to watch the ball right onto the racket. But we should aim to watch it until it reaches a point six to eight inches from the racket. I know this: when I'm not passing the opponent as he comes to the net I make up my mind to watch the ball that much more closely and invariably I meet with more success. It takes a conscious effort to watch the ball, and a lot of the oldsters who feel they can't see the ball well enough to carry on playing don't really make that effort.

Getting down to the ball, especially in making a low volley at the net, also presents a problem to the aging player who is not as slim as he was. I suggest that the player not discard the recognized principles of volleying, but that, as he takes the net position, he hold his racket at eye level and not down at his waist. He should also try to maneuver himself sideways to the net. If he does all this he should be able to dart to the forehand or the backhand and have his racket in a handy position to make a volley. So hold that racket up level with the eye and you'll find yourself getting down onto the right line for the lower balls.

One of the few advantages of age is that it usually brings a greater knowledge of strategy. However, as I have already said, all the strategy of a truly Machiavellian player will be of no avail against a good, highly trained young player. If a fellow is weak at the net, naturally you must try to bring him in to volley. You drop-shot him or play short balls. If he has a strong overhead smash you don't lob him. The smart player never feeds his opponent's strength.

Bound up with strategy is the psychological approach to the game. I am all in favor of gamesmanship so long as it is within the bounds of fairness. Part of the fun for the veterans is "psychoing" an opponent into a tough spot and thereby beating him. Here is an example of the importance of psychology. I played Bobby Riggs in a very close match at Newport, Rhode Island, when the temperature was around the century mark. I led two sets to one at the ten-minute rest period and I was extremely tired. But Riggs also was tired. In the locker room I overheard him tell his camp followers that he couldn't go on with the match. He was just not up to it. He was exaggerating, of course; he had no intention of forfeiting. However, he was pretty low and so I made out I was in much better physical condition. I hurried through my shower, put on new dry clothes and said loudly to a friend so that Riggs could hear: "Gee, I feel great—I can't wait to get out there again." That finished Riggs. I went through him fairly easily when we returned to the court.

At this point I will tell you of a piece of psychology, or rather philosophy, that helped me throughout my career as a tournament player and is as worthwhile now as ever. When I was eighteen I encountered a well-known player, who shall be nameless, coming off a court after losing a close match. "Well," he told a consoler, "if we had been playing on grass or clay I would have beaten that fellow. But cement isn't my surface at all. I couldn't be expected to win." I was young, interested in what the seasoned players had to say and impressionable. But I made my mind up then and there that I was not going to be one of those players who said, "If we had played under different conditions or on another day I would have won." In other words, I would never make an excuse for myself.

Therefore, I have felt very strongly since about any player alibiing because he didn't play on his home tennis or basketball court or football field, or because the wind was blowing or the ground was wet. Such an outlook has helped me immeasurably.

When I went to play in any championship, be it at Wimbledon, Forest Hills, Paris or Melbourne, I never looked at the draw because I didn't care whom I played. Each round was to be dealt with as it came. There was no sense in projecting my thoughts to the round of sixteen or to the quarter-finals. Once I did that, sure enough somebody would knock me off. And anyway it was an insult to any of my opponents to look beyond them. On any given day I might have a cold, or be otherwise off-color, or my opponent might run extra hot. It might be all I could do to get past him.

This approach, I am sure, is the best one for the older players as well as for the ambitious young tournament players. Don't complain about the conditions. Use them to the best of your ability. Tackle each match separately as it comes and assess each opponent on the merits he shows you, not on his reputation.

Should someone getting on in years attempt to play lawn tennis on hot days? This is another question that can be answered only by the individual. He knows best what kind of condition he's in and whether it's good enough to withstand a hard match under a hot sun. It follows that if you feel you are in better condition than the other fellow the hotter the day the quicker he is going to wilt. It may be that the sun will prove your ally and that after eight or ten games you will run through your flagging opponent easily.

The sensible player tries to conserve his energy on any day, but especially on hot days. In fact, conserving energy is one of the most important considerations for those over fifty. As I pointed out at the start of this chapter, they shouldn't try to run down balls they honestly feel they haven't a chance of reaching. That is energy-wasting and stupid and will result in matches being lost that, with finer judgment and greater conservation of strength, might have been won.

Try to relax between points and between games. Take your time about the court, and don't allow your opponent to rush you into resuming play before you're poised ready.

What if a player becomes tired in the middle of a set? What should his tactics be then? Well, he must use the score as a barometer. If the score is 3-all or 4-all he can't simply give the game up, because he has invested too much energy in getting to that stage. He has no choice. He must go all-out in an endeavor to win that set and hope that he can do it without being drawn into advantage games. Assuming he wins that set, he can coast. He may still manage to hold his own in the second set, but if he drops the first two or three games I should advise him to let that set go and concentrate on the third one. He will at least have an even chance of winning the third set if he has not exerted himself in the second. But, at 3-all or 4-all, a player has too great a stake in any set to let it go without a fight.

Theoretically, nobody should ever throw games if he's in excellent condition, though, as I say, if he's won the first set and is several games down in the second it might pay for him to go easy. I don't mean he should blatantly throw the set. He should try consciously to save energy while at the same time making his opponent run as much as he can. When you are in a situation such as this, drop-shot and lob your opponent. Even though you realize you are not going to win the set—that it is going to be one set all—you are not surrendering control. In the third set, if you've done your job properly and your opponent is tired by the effort he's made, you will have the edge.

Players of all ages should lob as much as they can. Remember, when a lob goes up a man has to spend a fair amount of energy in smashing it overhead for a winner. Ideally, shots should be mixed up—lobs, passing shots, drop shots—so that the other guy doesn't know quite what to expect. But lobs ought to be used even when they are expected because they tire an opponent and can well mean the difference betwen winning and losing a match.

As for the older player trying to cope with lobs, he should try to put them away if he feels confident enough. A deep lob, on the other hand, should be allowed to bounce and be smashed safely to the opponent's backhand or weaker corner in the hope of drawing an easier shot next time.

There are a few bad habits I feel everyone ought to shun, whether he is young or old. One is the tendency of players with weak backhands to run around their backhands and take the ball on their forehands. Once in a while, it does no harm. The service may be anemic, just asking to be pasted. But when a player runs around his backhand he leaves much of the court wide open. If his adversary has any competence at all, he is going to direct his shot into that open space.

The other bad habit is the chop, which, unfortunately, is seen quite frequently in club tennis. It is a defensive shot, and if you've learned the fundamental strokes well you should be able to do without it. I'm all in favor of offensive shots in every class of tennis. And I think if you make up your mind to play the offensive game, instead of piddling around with defensive chops, you will derive more pleasure and win more matches. The champions always have an offensive, positive attitude to their matches. They are competitors in the true meaning of the word.

Can the players of fifty and over maintain the same competitive edge? I think much of the fun in any game is being competitive—having the will to win and winning. There is no reason why older players, evenly matched, shouldn't give themselves wholeheartedly to the task of winning. Of course, somebody has to lose. Nobody wants to, but the game wouldn't be much fun if the possibility didn't exist. Provided you are fit, play the game for all the good it's worth. Be competitive. And always try to win.

I'm asked sometimes which part of an aging champion gives way first—his legs, his lungs, his eyes, his reflexes. I feel definitely it's his stomach muscles, because if these are strong the legs and the arms will keep going. That is the meaning of the old expression that a player has "a lot of guts." He is tough in the tummy, and so he can twist and turn, stretch and leap, and keep his legs going. If he can keep his legs going he can keep running—unless he is an excessive smoker.

So keep your stomach muscles in good shape and you may find it's worth a point a game. Floor exercises can be useful. Otherwise, keep a check on your diet, avoiding fatty foods that add inches to your waistline. It is always harder taking the inches off than putting them on.

Let me sum up by reverting to my original contention that age is no bar to enjoying lawn tennis provided one doesn't set one's sights on the unattainable. Let's face it. When people reach a certain age they don't move as well as the youngsters do. Perhaps, if they've had any kind of coaching in the fundamentals and training, they hit the ball as well. But they simply can't run as well. Stroke equipment is no replacement for strength and stamina.

On the other hand, be fundamentally correct in your strokes, use your common sense and adopt a good, healthy philosophy to the game. And you will not only wind up winning lots of matches. You will have loads of fun.

Tony Trabert
The Complete
Lawn Tennis Player

Champion lawn tennis players never increase their difficulties by using second-rate equipment or by taking thoughtless risks with their physical condition. With experience, they learn how to cope with the little problems that inevitably occur in even the best-ordered lives. We professionals, appreciating that the game is our livelihood, take great care of the incidentals—our rackets, our practice sessions, the injuries that may befall us and what we can do, if anything, to avoid them. In this chapter I will cover some of the details that the complete lawn tennis player mustn't overlook.

At the outset, let me say that the importance of good equipment cannot be stressed enough. If you play the game ambitiously the purchase of inferior rackets, tennis balls or clothing is false economy.

In selecting a racket the first requirement is that it should feel comfortable, being neither too heavy nor too light. A racket too heavy for you may well strain your shoulder or give you tennis elbow.

My racket, when strung, weighs fourteen ounces and has a five-inch grip, the largest on the circuit. That's because I am a big man. The average player should ask his club professional or nearest coach to help him select an evenly balanced racket that suits his physical make-up.

The tension of the racket strings also depends on the individual's physique, as well as on the surface of the court. When playing on clay courts, or courts which give a similarly slow bounce, I like to have my rackets strung medium tight—approximately sixty-two pounds of pressure. On faster surfaces such as grass, wood, cement or canvas, I prefer my rackets very tight, almost "board tight." My reasoning is this: On a slow surface you have to generate pace on the ball and you need your racket strung a little looser to give a sort of "sling-shot" effect. The ball sinks into the gut a little more before being propelled. On a faster surface the ball skids through as it hits the court and your job is to use that speed and control it. I find that a tight racket gives me all the pace I require and better control.

All top-class players prefer their rackets to be strung with gut rather than nylon. Gut puts more life into a racket. Players can get more pace on the ball while at the same time having what we call "better feel." And for delicate strokes—drop volleys and so on—you must have good "feel" to have any chance of success.

With gut in his racket, a player can hit a ball off-center and still have good results. On a grass court, where the bounce is often irregular, the ball is frequently hit off-center, and gut is essential.

Nylon certainly has some advantages. It lasts longer than gut and is not badly affected by dampness, whereas gut, used for instance on a grass court on a wet day, is ruined. The gut swells and the racket has to be restrung. Nylon in the same conditions would not deteriorate.

In 1951 Wilson Sporting Goods Company in Chicago asked me to play with nylon-strung rackets that they were interested in marketing. I won several important tournaments with them on clay and felt that at that time, when my big need was not pace

A study in grim concentration, Tony Trabert steps in to make a volley in front of his body, his racket head held solidly above his wrist.

but accuracy, they helped me. I was more consistent with nylon than with gut.

To the best of my knowledge, nylon is supplied in only one gauge or thickness, whereas gut comes in several. Most tournament players use what is known as sixteen light gauge, or sixteen medium, or sixteen heavy. I use sixteen heavy, the thickest gut, because I feel it gives me better control and lasts longer. If I were to give a categorical advice on this subject I would say that the tournament player and very good club player should use gut, while the average club player down to the beginner should use nylon.

No one looks after a racket with greater care than we professionals. As we have to travel to far-flung places where good rackets are not always obtainable, we each carry up to six. When not in use they are kept in racket covers, which keep the gut dry, and we carry them everywhere ourselves as a precaution against theft or loss. Normally, we don't throw our rackets around or test their bouncing quality on the court!

Racket presses would make the rackets too bulky for world travel, but I certainly recommend that you keep your rackets in both a cover and a press to prevent the frame from warping. Rackets are not cheap by any means, though because of better wood, lamination and glue, and their general construction, they are superior to the models our fathers and grandfathers had to use.

Often I see players practicing with old tennis balls, no doubt because they or their club can't afford new ones all the time. It's advisable, however, to use new balls whenever possible, because old balls feel and behave differently from the balls you use in a match. The same principle applies to golf. I remember once going out onto a practice fairway with Cary Middlecoff, who emptied a bag full of practice balls onto the turf. They were all new!

Fairly recently some "pressureless" tennis balls have been brought on the market. The few times I have used them I felt that in general they were satisfactory, but they felt just a fraction heavy, and it was a little more difficult to execute "touch" shots with them. I had to hit the "pressureless" ball a trifle harder than the regular ball in order to get the same depth on my shot. Technically, I understand, the ball is not totally without air pressure; it has merely been reduced to a minimum. Top tournament players prefer the regular ball, which has normal pressure, but in a few years' time there may be improvements to make them change their minds.

While on the subject of tennis balls, I will explain the usual strategy that's observed when new balls are taken during a match. On grass the balls pick up grass stain and become heavy. It's an advantage, therefore, to serve with new balls, for they will travel faster and skid through lower. Remembering that the new balls are lighter, the receiver must try to lower his trajectory, maybe shortening his backswing to tighten control. On cement and clay courts tennis balls become lighter as continual friction with the court surface rubs the nap from them. It follows that the new balls are heavier, allowing the players to exercise greater control, hitting the balls a little harder, but still keeping them in court.

Of the clothing a player needs, the most important is footwear. Every professional athlete makes sure that his feet are as comfortable as possible, because if he can't move about freely he's beaten from the start. Always wear proper-fitting tennis shoes with adequate support and thick woolen socks that absorb perspiration. I use only one pair of thick socks, but many players wear a thin cotton sock under their woolen sock in the belief that two socks provide a better cushion for the feet. Care has to be taken that there are no wrinkles in the cotton sock or you may get blisters.

In the professional troupe foot blisters are not common. They occur mainly when we come off grass or clay courts and go onto cement. We overcome the difficulty by taping the balls of our feet with moleskin, which has a flat backing and gives us the necessary protection.

Tennis clothes are a matter of personal preference, the main consideration being comfort and freedom of movement. Since the game is mostly played in warm weather, clothes should be fairly light in weight. Jockey caps used to be popular several years ago, but now most of the professionals don't wear any type of cap. We feel that on a hot day the peak of a cap tends to keep the hot air close to one's face and that it's more essential to have fresh air. If it's exceptionally hot the fellows may wear a floppy hat and, perhaps, even soak it with water in an effort to keep themselves cooler.

Sweaters, of course, are necessary, as they help a player to warm up at the start of a match and prevent him from getting a chill at the end of it. The body cannot perform efficiently until it is warm, and before a match we usually do warming-up exercises in the locker room. Some time earlier we try to hit tennis balls for a half hour or so, loosening up the muscles that probably have become a little stiff on a long car or plane journey. When you've been around in big tennis for a while you realize how badly you can hurt yourself by running or serving hard before you are really warm. A pulled muscle can put you out of the game for weeks.

Of course, injuries and ailments are likely to hit the most cautious of us, but we can try to cut down the risks as far as possible. The particular hazard that has menaced me from 1954 onward is blisters on my racket hand. They are, I can assure you, no fun. I checked with all kinds of doctors in the hope that someone would come up with a remedy. No one ever did. I had to face it: my skin blistered easily. So I simply taped up the affected parts of my hand and made myself get accustomed to the tape. There are various preparations you can buy to toughen up blistered skin. It is better, however, if you've had a lay-off, not to play too much too soon and to build your hand up gradually. Then you won't get blisters.

Cramps, sprains and pulled muscles have stopped many a player from carrying off a trophy for which he was favorite. I don't know that much can be done to avoid these misfortunes. There is always some element of physical risk in all vigorous sports.

By and large, a fit player won't be troubled too often by cramp, though all of the champions have suffered at least a twinge or two in their careers, either through playing in an extremely tense match on a hot day or through the match's being long and grueling. Earl Buchholz was in good condition when he went through a bad period with cramps and the doctors couldn't really help him.

All you can do for a sprained ankle is tape it and soak it liberally in hot, then cold water, breaking down the metabolism. You have to build up the strength of the ankle slowly, making sure it is well supported. Even then, you can never be sure that in a moment of stress it won't break down again, as happened with the Aussie girl Jan Lehane in her match with Darlene Hard at the 1963 Wimbledon.

Pulled muscles, which usually occur on cooler days, need rest and heat treatment. But if you have a slightly pulled muscle and badly want to play in an important match you can dose it with red-hot ointment, or something similar, before going out on the court. The ointment will penetrate into the muscle, keeping it warm while you are out there.

A heavy fall in a match may shake you. If it does, don't try to be a hero. Take your time picking yourself up, and walk around, or if you're concerned about a knee or an ankle, bend down and do whatever you can to help yourself recover. You may, perhaps, need a towel to wipe away dirt. A fall on court is an accident and both your opponent and the umpire will be willing to give you time within reason to recover before resuming. A lot of points can be sacrificed and a match lost by acting the hero and playing on while still groggy from a fall.

The consumption of pills other than salt tablets I do not advocate. The secret with salt pills, which are surely beneficial on a hot day, is not to wait until the match, but to take a couple two or three hours beforehand. Most good players make sure they have a lot of salt with their meals, realizing that otherwise, in hot weather, the salt they lose in their perspiration will weaken them.

As for any other pills, if a player thinks he needs them he should consult his physician, not a tennis pro. I have yet to come across anyone so nervous, for instance, that he needed a tranquilizer. A tranquilizer wouldn't help him to win anyway, because in a tight match a player needs all the nervous energy he can muster; a depressant would act against him. Everybody suffers from nerves, even the Hoads and Lavers. Normally when they're out on the court warming up or playing, the butterflies fly away. A symptom of nervousness is bad breathing. A player will puff and blow rapidly after only the slightest exertion if he's affected by tension. He can try deep breathing as one means of settling his nerves, but overcoming nervousness is really a matter of character and self-control. Most players, once they have started a match, will relax.

During a protracted match on a hot day there is a temptation to consume liquid, which I feel should be resisted. In my amateur days when I played long, difficult matches I never put any liquid into my stomach, though at the change of ends I might have swilled some water to remove what we call the "cotton" from my mouth. The consumption of cold liquid when the body's temperature is high will not only produce heaviness in the stomach, but also may shock the system. Warm tea, or something sweet and energy-giving may be O.K. But generally I think players are best advised to stay away from liquids in a match.

Some people say that they will never bet on a sweating horse, a theory that, whatever its merit in racing, certainly has no application to lawn tennis. When I was in the peak of physical condition I still perspired heavily, unlike other fit players who perspired very little. I guess you can't generalize. Perspiration can be irritating, but it is something that has to be put up with. Apart from wearing a sweatband on the wrist to prevent perspiration from running onto the racket hand and to mop up perspiration on the forehead, a towel should be left by the courtside for wiping the face and arms during the change of ends. A few players also keep a little supply of sawdust in their pocket to improve their grip on the racket if their hand gets too moist.

On occasions massage is beneficial, though it's unwise to develop an overreliance on it. In my Davis Cup days we had a masseur with the team and after each day's workout some of the fellows had a rubdown. I finally decided that this was making me a little sluggish and I felt physically better when I ceased being massaged. Most of the professionals have a steam bath and massage from time to time when they have a day free from tennis, but none make a ritual of the practice.

If you are going to be a top-flight player you ought to play tennis every day of the week. Provided you are in top condition, you don't really need a rest when you love what you are doing. A long lay-off can put a fellow way behind his rivals.

The professionals like to play almost continuously, although after a long, exacting tour, they may take a short rest and then resume practicing, with nothing at stake except possibly a side bet. Once you get up in years naturally it becomes increasingly harder to maintain condition and form, and a lay-off shouldn't be for too long.

The immediate hour or so before a vital tournament match should be spent relaxing. If, for instance, the program starts at two o'clock and you are scheduled to play in the second match, you can reckon to be on court about three o'clock or three-thirty, depending on whether the matches are being decided over three sets or five.

I would eat about twelve o'clock and go out to the courts unhurriedly. For a while I would watch the first match, then I would get away from the tennis, away from the sun, and find a

The complete tennis player has to keep blasting away even on a 90-degree summer day, when all the spectators are sitting quietly in shirt-sleeves. Here, deep in the third set of a long, hard match, Tony Trabert's condition and equipment stand up to the test.

nice quiet corner of the locker room. Somebody would keep me abreast of the situation outside and when the other match was nearing its end I would dress and go out into the sun to readjust my eyes to the bright light.

As an amateur I used to try to keep myself busy in the period just before a big match. I would write some letters, go for a walk, do a little shopping, get some fresh air—anything that wasn't tiring, but that would keep my mind occupied and prevent any undue tension building up.

As in other sports in which the protagonists are at a fine nervous pitch, needling is sometimes resorted to. I don't go along with it at all. Your aim should be to beat the other fellow with only those weapons at your disposal that are ethical. Talking to an opponent to upset him, or stalling, is unfair and an unsatisfactory way of winning. I never wanted to try it on anyone, and I never wanted anyone to try it on me. That goes for gamesmanship generally. A few good players have used gamesmanship, but the champions don't need to. It is totally unnecessary and unsportsmanlike, a virtual admission that you lack the shots to do the job properly.

We professionals have an understanding that we will do our level best at all times. Before an important match opponents say to each other, "Let's take all the calls as they come." Inevitably, there will be bad calls, but they will even out over the match. It is ludicrous to expect one man who has had some unexpected luck to throw the next point to his opponent. Occasionally, I've played against one of my best pals who perhaps has been ill and unable to produce his best form. I've felt obliged to beat him as badly as I can—and feel sorry for him afterward. He would pay me the same compliment if the positions were reversed.

With such a philosophy, we become the keenest competitors on court, while maintaining our friendship and respect for each other off the court.